FINANCE AND THE INTERNATIONAL ECONOMY
5

The Prize Winning Essays from the first four competitions have been published in the following Oxford University Press volumes:

Finance and the International Economy (The 1987 Essays)
eds. John Calverley and Richard O'Brien

International Economics and Financial Markets (The 1988 Essays)
eds. Richard O'Brien and Tapan Datta

Finance and the International Economy: 3 (The 1989 Essays)
eds. Richard O'Brien and Ingrid Iversen

Finance and the International Economy: 4 (The 1990 Essays)
eds. Richard O'Brien and Sarah Hewin

Finance and the International Economy

5

The AMEX Bank Review
Prize Essays

In Memory of
Robert Marjolin

Edited by
RICHARD O'BRIEN

PUBLISHED BY OXFORD UNIVERSITY PRESS

For The AMEX Bank Review

1991

Oxford University Press, Walton Street, Oxford OX2 6DP

Oxford New York Toronto
Delhi Bombay Calcutta Madras Karachi
Petaling Jaya Singapore Hong Kong Tokyo
Nairobi Dar es Salaam Cape Town
Melbourne Auckland

and associated companies in
Berlin Ibadan

Oxford is a trade mark of Oxford University Press

Published in the United States
by Oxford University Press, New York

British Library Cataloguing in Publication Data
Data available

Library of Congress Cataloging in Publication Data
Finance and the International Economy: 5,
The AMEX Bank Review prize essays in memory
of Robert Marjolin edited by Richard O'Brien.
Bibliography: p.7
1. International economic relations. 2. International finance.
3. Marjolin, Robert.
I. Marjolin, Robert. II. O'Brien, Richard. III. The AMEX Bank Review.
ISBN 0–19–828766–6

Set by Hope Services (Abingdon) Ltd.
Printed in Great Britain by Biddles Ltd.,
Guildford and King's Lynn

The AMEX Bank Review Awards
In Memory of Robert Marjolin

The AMEX Bank Review Awards are given annually in memory of Professor Robert Marjolin, the first head of the OECD (at that time the OEEC) and Vice-President of the European Commission for the first ten years of the European Community's existence. Professor Marjolin was one of the key architects of the Community and instrumental in establishing international economic cooperation in the post-war period. From 1975 to 1986 he was Editorial Adviser to *The AMEX Bank Review*. The Awards were launched in 1987 to promote new writing and analysis on current international economic and financial issues.

Robert Marjolin was one of the most distinguished European economists and public servants of his generation. He was a very practically minded economist, being more interested in achieving progress than advocating any one particular economic theory or dogma. In 1989 the English language edition of Robert Marjolin's memoirs, under the title *Robert Marjolin: Architect of European Unity* was published by Weidenfeld and Nicolson. As *The Economist* wrote in its review of these memoirs,

Robert Marjolin is a name that will ring bells in many people's minds but come into focus in few of them. Intellectually too honest either to be a forceful politician or to have the unreasonable convictions that take men to fame, he remained an *eminence grise* in postwar Europe.

For our part we would like to record our appreciation of Robert Marjolin's wise and friendly advice which was a constant encouragement in attempting to interpret current economic events. The Awards are judged by a special committee of bankers, economists and politicians, which in 1991 included: Professor Raymond Barre, former Prime Minister of France and former Vice President of the European Commission; Lord Roll of Ipsden, President of S. G. Warburg Group plc; Toyoo Gyohten, former Vice Minister of Finance for International Affairs, Japan, John Flemming, Chief Economist, European Bank for Reconstruction & Development, Professor Rudiger Dornbusch, Massachusetts Institute of Technology, USA, Rupert Pennant-Rea, Editor, The Economist, Bruce MacLaury, President of the Brookings

Institution, Washington DC; Kevin Pakenham, Chief Executive of the London investment group, John Govett & Co. Limited; and Richard O'Brien, Chief Economist of American Express Bank Ltd. and Editor of the *Review*. Both Mr MacLaury and Mr Pakenham are Editorial Advisers to the *Review*. The Bank is most grateful for the major contribution of the committee members in judging this competition.

The 1991 Competition

The year 1991 was the fifth year of the competition, and 254 economists from 55 countries entered. As in all previous years, essays were on any subject in international economics of current relevance to financial markets.

Eleven prizes were awarded, of a total value of US$56,000. The awards for the first three essays were US$25,000, US$10,000 and US$5,000 respectively, with eight Special Merit Awards of US$2,000. Summaries of all essays were published in the November 1991 issue of *The AMEX Bank Review*.

The 1991 results were announced at a special presentation dinner at the Merchant Taylors' Hall, London, on 13th November 1991. The awards were presented by Toyoo Gyohten, former Vice Minister of Finance for International Affairs, Japan, continuing a tradition of presentations by highly distinguished guests, following Professor Raymond Barre, former European Commissioner Lord Cockfield, the Rt. Hon. Robin Leigh-Pemberton, Governor of the Bank of England, and Karl Otto Pöhl, President of the Deutsche Bundesbank. The dinner was presided over by Mr Richard Thoman, Chairman and co-Chief Executive Officer of American Express International and by Mr Steven Goldstein, President and Chief Executive Officer of American Express Bank Ltd.

The competition continues in 1992 and we look forward to another high quality level of entries, to ensure that the Awards continues as a worthy memorial to the work of Robert Marjolin.

Contents

Editor's Introduction

This book contains the full texts of the eleven prize-winning essays in *The 1991 AMEX Bank Review* Awards, the essay competition run by American Express Bank Ltd. in memory of Professor Robert Marjolin. The *Review* is the monthly international economics and financial publication of the Bank and is published in London.

The essay competition calls for contributions on any subject in international economics and finance and thus covers a variety of issues. There is no pre-set subject. For presentation purposes, however, this volume publishes the eleven essays in groups as appropriate.

The *first* group, headed by the first and second prize winning essays, focuses on trade bloc issues, asking whether a yen bloc is emerging, whether trade blocs are to be welcomed or discouraged and whether growth maximisation by Japanese firms offers some explanation for their international competitiveness. The *second group* focuses on the economic issues associated with the integration of Eastern Europe and the international economy. The opening essay in this group, winner of the third prize, examines the impact of the integration of east Germany into the Federal Republic and the impact on the Deutschmark. Further papers examine the choice of exchange rate policy, inflation issues, and the relationship between the European Community and Eastern European nations. The *final group of essays* covers a series of different subjects, notably on information flows and the bank-corporate relationship, the impact of information technology on international financial markets, the need for sequencing in relaxing capital controls in developing economies and a lively discussion of the competing theories of asset market pricing behaviour.

While the essays vary in style, from empirical analysis through to more theoretical work, each essay draws out clear conclusions for policymakers or for the markets.

Essay Selection

These essays were chosen from 254 entries from 55 countries. In the selection process the judges were looking for several characteristics in the essays. Of particular importance was the extent of new thinking or research, though well-written essays bringing together more familiar but complex issues continued to fare well in the judging process. Stress was also placed upon the ability of authors to draw out clear conclusions and recommendations from the analysis.

Prize Winners' Forum

For the second year, all prize winners have been invited to debate their ideas at a public seminar: the 1991 Prize Winners' Forum was hosted by the Royal Institute for International Affairs, Chatham House, London, on November 14th 1991.

All the essays are published in the form in which they were submitted to the competition, with only minor changes. Short summaries and author biographies are presented with each essay. We are of course very pleased that all the essays continue to be published by Oxford University Press, this year's essays being published only two months after final revision.

We hope that the essays will provide stimulating reading on current issues in international economics and finance and, not least, encourage the submission of a further set of high quality entries, by scholars, public officials and private sector practitioners for the 1992 competition.

The Editor
The AMEX Bank Review

London
November 1991

Is a Yen Bloc Forming in Pacific Asia?

FIRST PRIZE

Summary

The essay reaches three conclusions regarding the Yen Bloc that Japan is reputed to be forming in East Asia and the Pacific. (1) Although growth in East Asian countries is rapidly raising their weight in world output and trade, the statistics do not bear out a movement toward intra-regional bias in trade and direct investment flows. (2) There is more evidence of rising Japanese influence in the region's *financial markets*. (3) Much of Japan's increasing financial influence takes place via a growing role for the yen in Asian countries' exchange rate policies and invoicing of trade and finance. But these trends are less the deliberate outcome of wishes on the part of Japanese policy-makers than of pressure from the US government to internationalize the yen.

Jeffrey A. Frankel is Professor of Economics at the University of California, Berkeley. He is also Associate Director for International Macroeconomics and Finance at the National Bureau of Economic Research in Cambridge, Massachusetts. From August 1983 to August 1984 he served at the President's Council of Economic Advisors in Washington. From July 1988 to January 1990 he was a Visiting Professor at the Kennedy School of Government, Harvard University. During the period when he wrote the present essay, he was a Visiting Scholar at the Institute for International Economics in Washington, DC. He has also had repeated visiting appointments at the International Monetary Fund and the Federal Reserve Board. Professor Frankel's research interests include international macroeconomic policy coordination, targets and indicators for monetary policy coordination, targets and indicators for monetary policy, the workings of the foreign exchange market, trade issues in Pacific Asia, the cost of capital in Japan, and worldwide financial market integration. Papers include 'International Macroeconomic Policy Coordination When Policy-Makers Do Not Agree on the Model', in the *American Economic Review*. Frankel is also the co-author (with R. Caves and R. Jones) of *World Trade and Payments* (5th edition, January 1990). He was born in San Francisco in 1952, graduated from Swarthmore College in 1974, and received his Ph.D. from MIT in 1978.

1

Is a Yen Bloc Forming in Pacific Asia?*

JEFFREY A. FRANKEL

Japan will be driven to form her own trade and finance zone in
Asia . . . The way Japan, Inc., operates also facilitates the
formation of an Asian co-prosperity zone: government and
business work hand-in-glove and business moves jointly . . . The
decision will be made by consensus, and the rest is routine.
(Dornbusch, 1989, p. 270)

The question 'Is Japan creating a Yen Bloc in the Pacific Asia?' is one
of those that is fun to pose, but unclear how to go about answering. We
read daily in the papers that the answer is 'yes': Japan is investing in
its neighbour countries on an unprecedented scale. Japanese subsidiaries in Asia export goods back to Japan in large quantities,
especially raw materials from Southeast Asia, and factories in Japan
are increasing their exports of advanced manufactures to pliant markets
in the rest of Asia. We are told that a self-contained trading bloc is
evolving along this edge of the Pacific, and the United States and
Europe face a choice between trying to stop the trend, or defensively
forming trade blocs of their own.

After examining some of the relevant statistics, this essay argues
that the evidence of an evolving East Asian trade bloc centred on Japan
is not so clear. Trade between Japan and other Asian countries
increased substantially in the late 1980s, but intra-regional trade
remains much smaller, for example, than trade within the European
Community. The phrase 'Yen Bloc' could, however, be interpreted as
referring to the financial and monetary aspects implicit in the words,
rather than to trade flows. The essay does find evidence of growing
Japanese influence in the Pacific via financial and monetary channels,
rather than primarily via trade flows.

* The author would like to thank Menzie Chinn for extremely efficient research
assistance.

One of the most remarkable and widely-remarked trends in the world economy over the last three decades is the rapid outward-oriented growth of Japan, followed by the four East Asian NICs (Newly Industrialized Countries) and subsequently by some of the other ASEAN countries (Association of South-East Asian Nations). But when one asks whether a yen bloc is forming in East Asia, one is presumably asking something more than whether trade and financial flows among these countries are increasing in absolute terms. One must ask whether the share of intra-regional trade and finance is higher, or increasing more rapidly, than would be predicted based on such factors as the GNP or growth rates of the countries involved.

Then, even if evidence were found that an economic bloc by this criterion was indeed forming, there would remain the separate question of whether this trend was the outcome of deliberate Japanese policy measures. Japan is, in fact, unusual among major countries in *not* having preferential trading arrangements with smaller countries. As for Japan's monetary power in the region, this essay concludes that if its policy-makers had their way, the internationalized yen might never have been unleashed.

A Trade Bloc in East Asia?

Table 1 decomposes trade (exports plus imports) undertaken by countries in East Asia into trade with other members of the same regional grouping, versus trade with other parts of the world. For comparison, the analogous statistics are reported for Western Europe (the EC Twelve) and for North America (the United States, Canada, and Mexico). Although such statistics depend very much on which years are chosen, the share of intra-regional trade in East Asia increased from 33 per cent in 1980 to 37 per cent in 1989. Pronouncements that a clubbish trade bloc is forming in the region are usually based on figures such as these. But the numbers are deceptive.

All three regions show increasing intra-group trade in the 1980s. The region that has both the highest and the fastest-increasing degree of intra-regional trade is not Asia but the European Community, reaching 59 per cent in 1989. The share of intra-regional trade in East Asia has not even been increasing appreciably faster than that in North America.

Quite aside from the comparison with Europe, it is easy to be misled by intra-regional trade shares such as those reported in Table 1. If one allows for the phenomenon that most of the East Asian countries in the 1980s experienced rapid growth in total output and trade, then it is likely that there has in fact been no movement toward intra-regional bias in the evolving pattern of trade. The increase in the intra-regional share of trade that is observed in Table 1 could be entirely due to the increase in economic size of the countries involved. To take the simplest case, imagine that there were no intra-regional bias in 1980, that each East Asian country conducted trade with other East Asian countries in the same proportion as the latter's weight in world trade (15%). Total trade undertaken by Asian countries increased by 108 per cent in dollar terms over this nine-year period, while total trade worldwide increased by only 53 per cent. Even if there continued to be no regional bias in 1989, the observed intra-regional share of trade would have increased by one-third (to 20%) due solely to the greater weight of Asian countries in the world economy

Table 1 Intra-regional vs. Inter-regional Trade in Three Blocs

	Billions of dollars			Fraction of total		
	1980	1986	1989	80	86	89
EAST ASIA						
Total trade	577.6	723.3	1199.6	1	1	1
Of which: Intrareg. Trade	189.2	234.3	448.1	.328	.328	.374
X + M from ROW	388.5	489.0	751.5	.673	.676	.626
X + M from N. America	127.7	223.2	330.6	.221	.308	.275
X + M from EC12	70.8	98.9	177.1	.122	.137	.148
EUROPEAN COMMUNITY 12						
Total trade	1517.7	1577.9	2299.5	1	1	1
Of which: Intrareg. Trade	768.6	896.7	1355.0	.506	.568	.589
X + M from ROW	749.2	681.2	954.5	.494	.432	.415
X + M from E. Asia	74.8	99.9	170.7	.049	.063	.074
X + M from N. America	132.6	150.9	205.0	.087	.096	.089
NORTH AMERICA						
Total trade	639.8	805.5	1145.1	1	1	1
Of which: Intrareg. Trade	207.0	279.5	415.7	.323	.347	.363
X + M from ROW	432.8	526.0	729.4	.676	.653	.637
X + M from E. Asia	116.3	218.3	317.8	.182	.271	.277
X + M from EC12	117.5	149.1	206.1	.186	.185	.180

Sources: Schott (1991) and *Direction of Trade*, International Monetary Fund.

Consider now the more realistic case where, due to transportation costs if nothing else, countries within each of the three groupings undertake trade that is somewhat biased toward trading partners within their own group (East Asia, North America, or the European Community). Although East Asian trade with other parts of the world increased rapidly, trade with other Asian countries increased even more rapidly. Does this mean that the degree of clubbishness or within-region bias intensified over this period? No, it does not. As in the so-called gravity models bilateral trade depends on the sizes of *both* trading partners.[1] *Even if there was no increase at all in the bias toward intra-Asian trade*, the more rapid growth of total trade and output experienced by Asian countries would show up as a rate of growth of intra-Asian trade that was faster than the rate of growth of Asian trade with the rest of the world.

Think of each East Asian country in 1980 as conducting trade with other East Asian firms in the same proportion as their weight in world trade (15%) multiplied by a regional bias term to explain the actual share reported in Table 1 (33%). Then the regional bias term would have to be 2.18 (=.33/15). An unchanged regional bias term multiplied by the East Asians' 1989 weight in world trade would predict that the 1989 intra-regional share of trade would be 44 per cent (2.18 × .20 = .436). The actual intra-regional share, however, did not increase to nearly this level. Thus the East Asian bias toward within-region trade, far from rising, actually diminished in the 1980s!

What about bilateral trade between Asian/Pacific countries and Japan? Like intra-regional trade overall, trade with Japan increased rapidly in the second half of the 1980s. Most of this increase merely reversed a decline in the first half of the 1980s however (Petri, 1991). More importantly, the recent trend in bilateral trade between Japan and its neighbours can be readily explained as the natural outcome of the growth in Japanese trade overall and the growth in trade levels attained by other Asian countries overall. Lawrence (1991) has calculated that, out of the 28 percentage point increase in the market share of Pacific Asian developing countries in Japanese imports from 1985 to 1988, 11 percentage points is attributable to improved competitiveness (as reflected in increased exports from Pacific Asia to worldwide markets), and 18 percentage points is attributable to the commodity mix of these countries' exports. There is no residual to be attributed to Japan's development of special trading relations with other countries in its region.

In short, beyond the evident facts that countries near each other trade with each other, and that Asian countries are growing rapidly, there is no evidence that they are concentrating their trade with each other in any special way, let alone that they are moving toward a trade bloc as rapidly (or as deliberately) as is Western Europe.

The Japanese Influence on Financial Flows in East Asia

In the case of financial flows, proximity is less important than it is for trade flows. For some countries the buying and selling of foreign exchange and highly rated bonds is characterized by the absence of significant government capital controls, transactions costs or information costs. In such cases, there would be no particular reason to expect greater capital flows among close countries than distant ones. Rather, each country would be viewed as depositing into the world capital pool, or borrowing from it, whatever quantity of funds it wished at the going world interest rate. Thus even if we could obtain reliable data on bilateral capital flows, and whatever pattern they happened to show, such statistics would not be particularly interesting.

Many Asian countries still have substantial capital controls, and financial markets that are in other respects less than fully developed. Even financial markets in Singapore and Hong Kong, the most open in Asia, retain some minor frictions. Where the links with world capital markets are obstructed by even small barriers, it is an interesting question to ask whether those links are stronger with some major financial centres than with others. This question is explored econometrically below.

Information costs exist for equities, and for bonds with some risk of default. These costs may be smaller for those investors who are physically, linguistically, and culturally close to the nation where the borrower resides. Proximity clearly matters as well in the case of direct investment, in part because much of direct investment is linked to trade, in part because linguistic and cultural proximity matter for direct investment.

Table 2 shows the figures for Japanese direct investment. The steady stream of direct investment by Japanese firms in East Asia has received much attention. But the table shows that, whether measured in terms of annual flows or cumulated stocks, Japan's direct investment in the region is approximately equal to its investment in Europe, and is much less than its investment in North America.[2]

Table 2 Japanese Foreign Direct Investment by Region

	FY 85	FY 86	FY 87	FY 88	Cumulative as of 1989
TOTAL	12.2	22.3	33.4	47.0	186.4
To E. Asia[a] $ billion	2.0	3.3	6.3	8.2	41.5
fraction	.164	.148	.189	.174	.223
To N. America[b] $ billion	5.5	10.4	15.4	22.3	75.1
fraction	.451	.466	.461	.474	.403
To ECc $ billion	1.9	3.5	6.6	9.1	30.2
fraction	.156	.157	.198	.194	.162

a. Includes People's Republic of China.
b. Excludes Mexico. (Cumulative Japanese FDI in Mexico totalled $1.7 billion in March 1989.)
c. Includes Switzerland.

Source: Schott (1991).

Similar statistics exist on Japanese portfolio investment. But, in the case of portfolio capital, looking at price data—that is, at interest rates—is more informative than looking at quantity data. For one thing, the quality of the data on interest rates is much higher than the quality of the data on capital flows. For another, the interest rate test is more appropriate conceptually. If the *potential* for arbitrage keeps the interest rate in a given Asian country closely in line with, say, Tokyo interest rates, then this constitutes good evidence of close links between the two national capital markets, even if the amount of actual arbitrage or other capital flow that takes place within a given period happens to be small.

Tokyo's Influence on Regional Financial Markets

Many East Asian countries have liberalized and internationalized their financial markets over the last ten to fifteen years.[3] A number of studies have documented Japan's removal of capital controls over the period 1979-84 by looking at the power of arbitrage to equalize interest rates between Tokyo and New York or London.[4] Australia and New Zealand, while lagging well behind Japan, also show signs of liberalization during the course of the 1980s.[5] Hong Kong and Singapore register impressively open financial markets, showing smaller interest differentials even than some open European countries like Germany (Hong Kong has long had open capital markets. Singapore undertook a major liberalization in 1978, though it has tried to segment its domestic money market from its offshore 'Asia dollar market').[6] Malaysia has officially liberalized, following Singapore,[7] though its covered differential has remained considerably higher.

We can apply a simple test to the hypothesis that a particular Asian country is dominated financially by Japan, versus the alternative hypothesis that ties to capital markets in the other industrialized countries are equally strong. We use the technique of OLS (Ordinary Least Squares) regression to see how the interest rate in a typical Asian country depends on interest rates in Tokyo and New York. Under the null hypothesis that the country's financial markets are insufficiently developed or liberalized to be directly tied to any foreign financial markets, the coefficients on foreign interest rates should be zero. Under the alternative hypothesis that the country's financial markets are closely tied to those in Tokyo, the coefficient on Tokyo interest rates should be closer to 1 than to 0; and similarly for New York.[8]

Table 3 presents estimates for three-month interest rates in Hong Kong and Singapore. For the Hong Kong interest rate, the influence of the New York market appears very strong; neither Tokyo, London nor Frankfurt has significant influence on average over the sample period (from 1976 to 1989). For the Singapore interest rate, the influence of New York is again very significant; but now there is also a significant, though smaller, weight on Tokyo. The evidence suggests that both countries have had open financial markets ever since the mid-1970s, with New York having the dominant influence, but with Tokyo also having a one-quarter effect in the case of Singapore.

To see whether the influence of the foreign financial centres changed

Table 3 Japanese, US, UK, and German Interest Rate Effects in Hong Kong and Singapore

	Hong Kong		Singapore	
	without trend	with trend	without trend	with trend
Constant term	-2.41* (1.08)	-1.70 (1.13)	-1.16* (0.67)	-0.65 (0.67)
Tokyo effect	-0.23 (0.17)	-0.11 (0.69)	0.23** (0.07)	-0.36* (0.22)
Time trend in Tokyo effect		-0.00 (0.01)		0.02* (0.01)
New York effect	1.32** (0.15)	0.61 (0.52)	0.75** (0.09)	0.65* (0.33)
Time trend in New York effect		0.01 (0.01)		0.00 (0.01)
London effect	0.10 (0.11)	1.38** (0.47)	-0.07 (0.06)	-0.09 (0.16)
Time trend in London effect		-0.03** (0.01)		-0.00 (0.00)
Frankfurt effect	0.14 (0.20)	-1.74* (1.13)	0.19 (0.12)	1.02* (0.54)
Time trend in Frankfurt effect		0.04* (0.02)		-0.02* (0.01)
R^2	.83	.85	.87	.88
D.W.	1.50	1.61	1.53	1.92
Sample period	1976/4 to 1989/3		1974/1 to 1988/1	

* Statistically significant at 90 per cent significance level.
** Statistically significant at 99 per cent significance level.
(Standard errors reported in parentheses.)

over the course of the sample period, we can allow for time trends in the coefficients, also reported in Table 3. For Hong Kong, it is clear that London used to have a strong influence, and equally clear that the British influence has been diminishing over time. For Singapore, there is no sign of change in New York's role, but there is weak evidence of a role for Frankfurt that has been gradually diminishing over time, and of a gradually increasing role for Tokyo.

Similar tests were also run for four other Pacific countries: Australia, New Zealand, Taiwan and Korea (not reported here, to save space). There is evidence of a London effect in Australia that has been slowly increasing during the sample period, and a Frankfurt effect in New Zealand that gave way to a Tokyo effect late in the sample period.

For purposes of comparison we can look at developments in Europe (also not reported here). Similar regressions for European countries show that Frankfurt has, for example, a substantial effect in Switzerland, a rapidly increasing role in Denmark and Norway, and a significant and increasing role in Austria.[9]

Overall, there is only weak evidence in Table 3 of a special role for Tokyo as a financial centre exerting influence in its part of the world. But during most of the sample period examined, most Asian countries had not yet opened their financial markets to external influence by *any* foreign centre.

These first tests leave some important questions unanswered. First, what would such tests show for the last three years? Economic relationships have been changing rapidly in international financial markets. Korea and Taiwan, for example, have begun to liberalize and internationalize only very recently. Second, are the barriers that remain between a given country and the major world financial centres due to currency factors or country factors? Most of the Asian countries experience frequent changes in their exchange rates against the yen and the dollar. Financial markets in a country like Singapore could be very open and yet observed interest rates could differ from those in Tokyo or New York because of premia meant to compensate investors for the possibility of changes in the exchange rate. The question of whether the yen is playing an increasing role in the exchange rate policies of East Asian countries is an important one to address, but it should be kept distinct from the question whether financial links to Tokyo (irrespective of currency) are strengthening.

Table 4 analyses the determination of interest rates in five Pacific countries with monthly data for a more recent time period: 1988-91.

Jeffrey A. Frankel

Table 4 Japanese and US Interest Rate Effects in Five Pacific Countries, 1988-91

Regression of local interest rate against:
1) Japanese and US interest rates
2) Japanese and US interest rates adjusted for expectations of exchange rate changes as reflected in *Currency Forecasters' Digest*
3) Japanese and US interest rates adjusted for forward discount

		Constant term	Tokyo effect	New York effect	R^2	D.W.
Singapore	1)	-2.29**	0.82**	0.43**	.85	0.53
		(0.84)	(0.07)	(0.09)		
	2)	3.30**	-0.01	0.27**	.71	0.43
		(0.39)	(0.03)	(0.05)		
	3)	1.47**	0.29**	0.41**	.72	1.41
		(0.45)	(0.05)	(0.06)		
Australia	1)	-6.66**	0.74**	2.11**	.73	0.19
		(2.32)	(0.18)	(0.26)		
	2)	13.90**	0.10*	-0.07	.03	0.20
		(1.40)	(0.06)	(0.12)		
	3)	3.83**	0.07	0.67**	.76	1.36
		(1.13)	(0.21)	(0.20)		
Taiwan	1)	-4.93	1.91**	0.32	.53	1.17
		(4.04)	(0.32)	(0.45)		
	2)	7.14	0.07	0.10	.05	0.82
		(0.67)	(0.08)	(0.12)		
Korea	1)	-4.08*	1.29*	1.16**	.69	0.78
		(2.33)	(0.19)	(0.26)		
	2)	11.65**	0.04	0.27**	.55	1.28
		(0.32)	(0.04)	(0.07)		
Hong Kong	1)	-6.40**	0.25*	1.66**	.79	0.59
		(1.51)	(0.15)	(0.17)		

*Statistically different from zero at 90% significance level.
** Statistically different from zero at 99% significance level.
(Standard errors are reported in parentheses.)

There is more evidence of an important role on the part of Tokyo than there was in the earlier period. For Singapore, where the influence of Tokyo in Table 3 was less than New York but rising over time, estimates in the first row 1, based simply on interest rates, suggest that the Japanese financial centre has now surpassed its American rival. For Taiwan, Tokyo dominates so strongly that New York doesn't even seem to matter. For Hong Kong and Australia, on the other hand, New York dominates. For Korea, the two major financial centres appear to be equally strong.

As noted above, a country could have close financial ties with a foreign country and yet, if exchange rate changes are important, the simple regression against the foreign interest rate would be inappropriately designed to show this relationship. We can take out currency factors by using the forward exchange market. We simply express the foreign interest rates so as to be 'covered' or hedged against exchange risk. Doing so in Table 4 changes the results for Australia and Singapore toward a Tokyo effect that is smaller than the New York effect.[10] (Usable forward rate data are not available for the other countries.)

For four of these countries, there exists another way of correcting for possible exchange rate changes: direct data on forecasts of market participants collected in a monthly survey by the *Currency Forecaster's Digest* of White Plains, NY.[11] One advantage of using the survey responses to measure expected exchange rate changes is that the data allow us to test explicitly whether there exists an exchange risk premium that creates an international differential in interest rates even in the absence of barriers to international capital flows. Such a differential would be compensation to risk-averse investors for holding assets that they view as risky.[12] An advantage of the *Currency Forecasters' Digest* data in particular is that they are available even for countries like Taiwan and Korea where financial markets are less developed. A potential disadvantage is the possibility that survey data measure the expectations of market participants imperfectly.

For Singapore, the survey data corroborate the finding from the forward rate data that, once expected depreciation is eliminated as a factor, the New York effect dominates the Tokyo effect. For Korea, the survey data also show that the Tokyo effect becomes smaller than the New York effect.

The Role of the Yen

The finding that eliminating exchange rate expectations from the calculation leaves Tokyo with relatively little effect on local interest rates in most of these countries does not mean that the Japanese influence is not strong. It is likely, rather, that much of the influence in the Pacific comes precisely through the role of the yen. If Pacific countries assign high weight to the yen in setting their exchange rate policies, then their interest rates will be heavily influenced by Japanese interest rates.

No Asian or Pacific countries have ever pegged their currencies to the yen in the post-war period. But neither are there any Pacific countries that the International Monetary Fund classifies as still pegging to the US dollar. (Hong Kong has since October 1983 followed a policy of pegging to the dollar,[13] but the colony is not an official member of the IMF.) Malaysia and Thailand, and a number of Pacific island countries, officially peg to a basket of major currencies and are thought to give heavy weight to both the dollar and yen, but the weights are not officially announced.

There is other evidence, however, that the yen is playing an increasing role in the region. As Table 5 shows, Asian central banks in the course of the 1980s increased their holdings of yen from 13.9 per cent of their foreign exchange reserve portfolios to 17.5 per cent.[14] The yen is also being used more widely to invoice trade and finance in Asia. The countries that incurred large international debts in the 1970s and early 1980s subsequently shifted the composition away from dollar-denominated debt and toward yen-denominated debt. Table 5 shows that the yen share among five major Asian debtors nearly doubled between 1980 and 1988, entirely at the expense of the dollar.[15]

Table 5 Share of the Yen in Debt-Denomination and Official Reserve Holidays

In per cent

	Yen share in external debt of five countries						Yen share in in official holdings	
	Indonesia	Korea	Malaysia	Phil.	Thailand	Total	Asia	World
1980	20.0	16.6	19.0	22.0	25.5	19.5	13.9	4.4
1981	19.3	14.1	16.9	20.6	23.2	17.8	15.5	4.2
1982	21.0	12.3	13.2	19.2	24.0	17.2	17.6	4.7
1983	23.3	12.5	14.2	20.0	27.3	18.5	15.5	5.0
1984	25.0	12.8	21.2	20.0	29.2	20.3	16.3	5.8
1985	31.7	16.7	26.4	24.9	36.1	25.8	26.9	8.0
1986	33.9	22.0	30.4	25.5	39.9	29.3	22.9	7.9
1987	39.4	27.2	35.7	35.2	43.1	36.0	30.0	7.5
1988	39.3	29.5	37.1	40.5	43.5	37.9	26.7	7.7
1989							17.5	7.9

* Selected Asian countries (not including Japan).
Source: Tavlas and Ozeki (1991).

We may draw three conclusions.

(1) Although growth in Japan, the four NICs, and other East Asian countries, is rapidly raising their weight in world output and trade, the statistics do not bear out a movement toward intra-regional bias of trade and direct investment flows. (2) There is more evidence of rising Japanese influence in the region's *financial markets*. Tokyo appears to have recently acquired a dominant influence over interest rates in Singapore and Taiwan. It also has important and increasing effects on interest rates elsewhere in the Pacific, though overall its influence is as yet no greater than that of New York. (3) Much of Japan's financial influence takes place through a growing role for the yen, at the expense of the dollar. The yen's importance in exchange rate policies and invoicing of trade and finance in the region is increasing.

This still leaves a question raised at the beginning of this essay. Are these trends the outcome of deliberate policy measures on the part of Japan? It is difficult to see, even with imagination, signs of deliberate policy actions taken by the Japanese government to increase its financial and monetary influence in Asia. To the contrary, at least until recently, the Japanese government has resisted any tendency for the yen to become an international currency in competition with the dollar. It has been the US government, in the Yen/Dollar Agreement of 1984 and in subsequent negotiations, that has been pushing Japan to internationalize the yen, to promote its worldwide use in trade, finance, and central bank policies.[16] It has also been the US government that has been pushing Korea and other East Asian NICs to open up their financial markets, thereby allowing Japanese capital and Japanese financial institutions to enter these countries. It has again been the US government that has been pushing Korea and Taiwan to move away from policies to stabilize the value of their currencies against the dollar.[17] The increasing role of the yen in Pacific Asia may or may not be a good idea. But it is an idea that originated in Washington, not in Tokyo.

References

Abidin, A. Z., 1986, 'Financial Reform and the Role of Foreign Banks in Malaysia', in *Financial Policy and Reform in Pacific Basin Countries,* Hanson Cheng, ed. (Lexington Books: Lexington, MA), pp. 305-309.

Argy, Victor, 1987, 'International Financial Liberalisation—The Australian and Japanese Experiences Compared', *Bank of Japan Monetary and Economic Studies* 5, 1, 105-168.

Balassa, Bela, and John Williamson, 1990, *Adjusting to Success: Balance of Payments Policy in the East Asian NICs*, Policy Analyses in International Economics 17 (Institute for International Economics: Washington, DC). Revised, April.

Dornbusch, Rudiger, 1989, 'The Dollar in the 1990s: Competitiveness and the Challenges of New Economic Blocs', in *Monetary Policy Issues in the 1990s* (Federal Reserve Bank of Kansas City).

Edwards, Sebastian and Mohsin Khan, 1985, 'Interest Rate Determination in Developing Countries: A Conceptual Framework', *IMF Staff Papers* 32, Sept., 377–403.

Frankel, Jeffrey, 1984, *The Yen/Dollar Agreement: Liberalizing Japanese Capital Markets*, Policy Analyses in International Economics no. 9 (Institute for International Economics: Washington, DC).

Frankel, Jeffrey, 1989, 'And Now Won/Dollar Negotiations? Lessons from the Yen/Dollar Agreement of 1984', in *Korea's Macroeconomic and Financial Policies* (Korean Development Institute: Seoul), December.

Frankel, Jeffrey, 1991a, 'Quantifying International Capital Mobility in the 1980s', in *National Saving and Economic Performance*, D. Bernheim and J. Shoven, eds. (University of Chicago Press: Chicago), 227-260. [To be adapted in Dilip Das, ed., *Current Issues in International Trade and International Finance* (Oxford University Press: Oxford, UK).]

Frankel, Jeffrey, 1991b, 'The Japanese Cost of Finance: A Survey', *Financial Management*, Spring, 95-127.

Frankel, Jeffrey, and Kenneth Froot, 1987, 'Using Survey Data to Test Standard Propositions Regarding Exchange Rate Expectations', *American Economic Review* 77, no. 1, March, 133-153. [To be reprinted in *Exchange Rate Economics*, edited by R. MacDonald and M. Taylor, International Library of Critical Writings in Economics (Edward Elgar Publishing, Cheltenham, UK).]

Glick, Reuven, 1987, 'Interest Rate Linkages in the Pacific Basin', *Economic Review* No. 3, pp. 31-42.

Glick Reuven, and Michael Hutchison, 1990, 'Financial Liberalization in the Pacific Basin: Implications for Real Interest Rate Linkages', *Journal of the Japanese and International Economies* 4, 36–48.

Ito, Takatoshi, 1986, 'Capital Controls and Covered Interest Parity', NBER working paper no. 1187, and *Economic Studies Quarterly* 37, 223-241.

Komiya, Ryutaro and Ryuhei Wakasugi, 1991, 'Japan's Foreign Direct Investment', *Annals of the American Academy of Political and Social Science*, Jan.

Krugman, Paul, 1991, 'The Move Toward Free Trade Zones', in *Policy*

Implications of Trade and Currency Zones, Federal Reserve Bank of Kansas City conference, Jackson Hole, Wyoming, August.

Lawrence, Robert, 1991, 'An Analysis of Japanese Trade with Developing Countries', Brookings Discussion Papers no. 87, April.

Moreno, Ramon, 1988, '*Exchange Rates and Monetary Policy in Singapore and Taiwan*', in *Monetary Policy in Pacific Basin Countries*, Hanson Cheng, ed. (Kluwer Press: Boston).

Noland, Marcus, 1990, *Pacific Basin Developing Countries: Prospects for the Future* (Institute for International Economics: Washington, DC).

Otani, I., and S. Tiwari, 1981, 'Capital Controls and Interest Rate Parity: The Japanese Experience', 1978-1981, *IMF Staff Papers* 28, 793-815, Dec.

Petri, Peter, 1991, 'Japanese Trade in Transition: Hypotheses and Recent Evidence', in *The United States and Japan: Has the Door Opened Wider?*, Paul Krugman, ed. (University of Chicago Press, Chicago), forthcoming.

Schott, Jeffrey, 1991, 'Trading Blocs and the World Trading System', *The World Economy* 14, no. 1, March, 1-17.

Tavlas, George and Yuzuru Ozeki, 1991, 'The Japanese Yen as an International Currency', IMF Working Paper WP/91/2, International Monetary Fund, Jan.

Notes

1 Krugman (1991) has made a crude first pass at applying the gravity model to the question whether Europe and North America are separate trading blocs, but did not get as far as including other countries, or including a variable for distance.

2 See also Komiya and Wakasugi (1991).

3 Frankel (1991a) presents the 1980s evidence for Japan, Australia, New Zealand, Singapore, Hong Kong and Malaysia.

4 These include Otani and Tiwari (1981), Ito (1986), and Frankel (1984). The interest rates in the calculations are covered on the forward exchange or Eurocurrency markets so as to avoid exchange risk.

5 The frequently large negative covered differential that had been observed for Australia up to mid-1983 (see, e.g., Argy, 1987) largely vanished thereafter.

6 See Moreno (1988). Edwards and Khan (1985) includes another test of covered interest parity for Singapore.

7 Abidin (1986) and Glick and Hutchison (1990, p. 45).

8 It should be noted that if capital markets in Tokyo and New York are closely tied to *each other*, as they indeed are (endnote 4), then multicollinearity might make it difficult to obtain statistically significant estimates. But this does not mean that there is anything wrong with the test. A finding that the

coefficient on the Tokyo interest rate is statistically greater than 0, or than the coefficient on the New York interest rate, remains valid.

9 It also has a significantly growing effect in France, Belgium, Denmark and Spain, if one uses the forward market to correct for the likelihood of exchange rate changes against the mark, as discussed below. (In the case of Denmark and Italy, Frankfurt's gain is at London's expense. London had a large effect in Belgium and Denmark early in the sample period and a large but rapidly diminishing effect in Italy.)

10 For the case of Australia, the coefficient on the covered foreign interest rate is close enough to 1 to constitute statistical support of the hypothesis that 'covered interest parity' holds. That is, capital controls and other barriers to the movement of capital between Sydney and New York are close to zero. (The Durbin-Watson statistics improve substantially when the forward rates are included, suggesting that the equation that uses covered interest rates is a more appropriate specification.)

11 The use of such data, obtained originally from a survey conducted by *The AMEX Bank Review* and later from surveys conducted by MMS International and others, was explored by Frankel and Froot (1987), for the case of five major currencies. The *Currency Forecaster's Digest* data is proprietary, and was obtained by subscription by the Institute for International Economics.

12 The forward rate data allow us to eliminate factors associated with the currency in which countries' assets are denominated, but they do not allow us to distinguish between two currency factors: the exchange risk premium and expectations of depreciation. For the case of Australia, for example, the support for covered interest parity (see endnote 10) suggests that barriers to the movement of capital between Sydney and New York are low, and so differences in interest rates are due to currency factors. But when the Australian interest rate is observed to exceed the US interest rate, is this because the Australian dollar is confidently expected to depreciate, or is it because investors have no idea what the exchange rate will do and demand to be compensated for this risk? The survey data may be able to distinguish between these two hypotheses, whereas the forward rate data cannot.

13 Balassa and Williamson (1990, p. 32).

14 The deutschmark and Swiss franc are the two currencies that suffered the largest loss in share in the region.

15 Tavlas and Ozeki (1991) give further statistics.

16 Frankel (1984).

17 Balassa and Williamson (1987), Noland (1990) and Frankel (1989). Financial negotiations between the US Treasury and the governments of Korea and Taiwan were a response to congressional passage of the 1988 Omnibus Trade Bill.

Emerging Regional Arrangements :
Building Blocks or Stumbling Blocks?

SECOND PRIZE

Summary

This paper challenges the view that increased regional integration will lead to a world of trading blocs with disastrous consequences for financial markets and the global economy. On the contrary, regional arrangements will complement and enhance multilateral efforts at global integration and help the renewal of capital flows to Latin America. Planned regional arrangements will offer major benefits to outsiders by stimulating growth and enhancing market forces. A single European market with effective disciplines on national policies affords benefits to non-European competitors. Free trade agreements with the US help Latin American liberalization to be credible and permanent. Thus current regionalization initiatives reflect radically different forces than those in the 1930s or in Latin America in the 1960s, entailing a competitive dynamic leading these arrangements to be inclusive rather than exclusionary. Regional arrangements also offer more credibility and more certain governance than the GATT can currently provide, something in which both businesses and markets can take heart. Nonetheless, increased regional integration need not undermine the GATT and extra-regional trading linkages are of vital importance for each of the three regions. All have become global traders with an interest in an open system. If, as they are likely to be, these arrangements are crafted as open and designed to reinforce rather than resist market forces, they will become building blocks rather than stumbling blocks in the trend towards a more integrated world economy.

Robert Z. Lawrence is Albert L. Williams Professor of International Trade and Investment at the John F. Kennedy School of Government, Harvard University. He received his BA in Economics from the University of Witwatersrand, South Africa (1970), his MA in International Relations (1973) and Ph.D. in Economics (1978) from Yale University. Previously a senior fellow in the Economic Studies Program at the Brookings Institution (1983–91), he has taught at Yale University and at the Johns Hopkins School of Advanced International Studies. He has served as a consultant to the Federal Reserve Bank of New York, the World Bank, the OECD and UNCTAD. He is a Nonresident Senior Fellow at Brookings, an advisor to the Institute for International Economics, the Panel on Foreign Trade Statistics of the National Academy of Sciences, and the Committee for Economic Development, and writes a monthly column for the *Nikkei Financial Journal*. His books include: *Can America Compete?*; *Saving Free Trade: A Pragmatic Approach*; and *Primary Commodity Markets and the New Inflation*. He has coedited *Barriers to European Economic Growth: A Transatlantic Perspective*; and *An American Trade Strategy: Options for the 1990s*.

2

Emerging Regional Arrangements:
Building Blocks or Stumbling Blocks?*

ROBERT Z. LAWRENCE

The spectre of global fragmentation is haunting the global trading system and with it international financial markets. The fear is that progress toward global integration over the past four decades will be reversed as the world economy splits up into three regional trading blocs, each centred on a major currency, each closed to outsiders. No one familiar with the history of the 1930s can forget what Charles Kindleberger has called the 'disarticulation of the world economy' in which multilateral trade was virtually confined to currency blocs, international capital markets dried up and the international adjustment mechanism failed to operate.[1] But concerns that this scenario could be repeated reflect a fundamental misreading of the evidence. The major regional initiatives currently under way are more likely to represent the building blocks of an integrated world economy than stumbling blocks which prevent its emergence. To be sure, there are risks that these initiatives could go astray. But the forces initiating these developments are the very opposite of protectionism. They represent positive, integrative responses to the pressures exerted by globalization. If accompanied by parallel progress at the GATT, regionalization could be a potent mechanism for freeing world trade and investment and harmonizing national institutional practices.

Stumbling Blocks?

Outsiders have fears about each of the regional initiatives currently under way. In this analysis I will outline some of these concerns and then indicate why they are misplaced.[2]

The European Community's Single Market Initiative (EC92) is viewed with concern because of fears that (i) this initiative will divert

* I owe this phrase to Jagdish Bhagwati.

more trade than it creates; (ii) as its membership grows, the EC will become increasingly preoccupied with internal concerns and thus neglect its external relations; and (iii) a more centralized European Community would be dominated by the preferences of its more protectionist members and erect new external barriers.

A second concern is that Japan will spearhead a Southeast Asian bloc, principally by moving its manufacturing industry offshore. The favourite analogy is to the migration of geese: Japan is the head goose, with a V-formation of newly industrialized countries (NICs) of Southeast Asia and China following (or expected to follow) closely behind.[3] This formation is motivated by the Japanese desire to exploit cheaper Asian labour to produce for Japan and elsewhere. As Japanese investment rises in other Southeast Asian countries, so goes this argument, Japan will obtain control over these rapidly growing markets, erecting invisible barriers that will make it difficult for other countries to penetrate. And acting through MITI, Japan supposedly will try to manage international specialization in a manner which inhibits the free entry of firms and products from outside the region.[4]

A third concern relates to US initiatives in the Western Hemisphere. One fear is that such an agreement could have substantial trade-diversion effects. A second is that, like the EC, the US would be diverted from global initiatives, which, given the major leadership role it has played in the post-war trading system, would be a major blow to liberalization.

Clearly, any turn inward by the EC or the US could have domino effects. A Fortress Europe would encourage non-European countries shut out of European markets to think about forming their own closed blocs among their neighbours. An Asian bloc run by Japan could topple the global trading system by increasing demands for managed trade.

Moreover, corporate responses to these regional arrangements could enhance global fragmentation. The threat of protection will induce major corporations to adopt multiregional strategies in which each region is served through local production facilities. Once foreign companies are located within a region, they are less vulnerable to trade barriers and thus less inclined to oppose them. Paradoxically, therefore, this form of corporate globalization could weaken, rather than strengthen trade liberalization.

In sum, the apparent movement toward blocs has generated concern among defenders of multilateralism. They fear that, at best, a proliferation of blocs will make future global liberalization more difficult, and at worst, lead to a new round of trade wars.

Building Blocks?

But many of these concerns are misplaced. Stronger regional integration need not be associated with higher external barriers. Indeed, as the GATT itself recognizes, such a trend could have positive effects on the rest of the world provided the emerging regional blocs are 'open' to trade from outside.

Growth. One key benefit to the rest of the world comes from the impact of regional arrangements in stimulating growth and thus demand for extra-regional exports. These growth effects stem from several sources. One is the income effect of the gains from trade. Secondly, such increased income induces increased investment. For example, Richard Baldwin estimates that the removal of trade and other internal barriers to trade and investment within Europe as part of the Single Market will stimulate sufficient increases in investment to produce 'dynamic' growth effects that will be greater than the 'static' efficiency gains: up to a 10 per cent increase in total output, as compared to the 4.5 per cent figure (for static gains alone) estimated in the official Cecchini report prepared for the Commission.[5] Another positive source of growth stems from the beneficial macroeconomic effects of these regional initiatives. 'Animal spirits' have a major impact on investment. The psychological impact of the 1992 initiative in shifting Europe from 'Europessimism' to 'Europhoria' should not be underestimated, nor should the impact of increased expected competition. European firms have been convinced that the post-1992 Europe will be different. To prepare themselves they have been investing and merging. Their behaviour is a striking contrast to their sluggish investment in the late 1970s and early 1980s. Regardless therefore of whether the final details of the internal market are actually completed, the changed competitive environment has already brought considerable growth benefits.

Similarly, the restoration of investor confidence is the key to economic recovery in Latin America. The credible integration of these economies with the USA and Canada is a vital mechanism for restoring this confidence. The improved ability to attract foreign investment will permit these countries both to restore growth and to return to their natural positions as nations with trade deficits. This shift will in turn provide increased export opportunities for all their trading partners, not simply those within the region.

Another key reason for benefits to Europe's trading partners stems from the sectoral location of the main benefits of the Single Market. The Single Market will probably make its most important contribution in introducing competition among firms in many of the sectors for goods and particularly for services which were formerly nontradable. While growth in Europe's traded goods sectors could improve or worsen the rest of the world's terms of trade—depending on whether it is biased toward imports or exports—growth in the nontraded goods sector is unambiguously good for the rest of the world, because it results in increased demand for imports.

External barriers. Open regional blocs can actually promote and facilitate external liberalization, that is, trade with parties outside blocs. On the political front, regions might be more willing to agree to liberalization than individual countries. The postwar experience with the EC is heartening. Increased European integration after the Treaty of Rome was quite compatible with the lowering of Europe's external barriers. Gary Hufbauer, for example, has argued that the Kennedy Round of trade negotiations would not have occurred in the absence of the EC. 'France and Italy, in particular, would have strongly resisted making any trade concessions in the 1960s, and Germany would not have made trade concessions in isolation from its continental partners.'[6] With the noteworthy exception of agriculture, therefore (an exception for which the EC was not solely to blame), increased regional integration among the original six members of the EC was associated with extensive participation in multilateral tariff reductions. Indeed the formation of the EEC was an important impulse for the Kennedy Round.

The European experience also demonstrates that excluded countries have stronger incentives to liberalize in a system with emerging regional arrangements. Instead of the fragmentation process some fear, an expansionary dynamic is likely. The prospects (indeed, the actuality) that major trading partners could move into arrangements from which they are excluded could well drive countries to join regional liberalization schemes. The EEC's formation, for example, set in motion a cumulative regional liberalization process in which the United Kingdom was initially induced to join EFTA and later the EC itself. For the numerous developing countries which once had close linkages to individual European nations through colonial ties, the EC provided a mechanism for extending these to Europe as a whole through the special arrangements which the Community has with ACP, Mediterranean, and Magreb countries. Similar pressures are now operating under the Single Market in which the EFTA nations, East Europeans and others such as Turkey are clamouring for inclusion.

As was the case with the EC, the North American Free Trade Agreement (FTA) also is not developing as an exclusive process. Indeed, as Mexico has moved into the FTA negotiations with the US it has simultaneously sought to counterbalance this growing dependence on its more powerful partners with new initiatives toward the Pacific, Central and South America. Mexico, is seeking, for example, to join the OECD, is negotiating another FTA with Venezuela and Chile, and has signed agreements to achieve freer trade with several Central American countries.

The United States has also not been able to confine its attention to Mexico. President Bush has invited other Western Hemisphere nations to sign FTAs with the US separately or as groups in his 'Enterprise for the Americas Initiative'. The pressures of being left out of a prosperous regional arrangement are inducing many countries to accept this invitation. But the dynamic effects are not confined to agreements with the United States. This US invitation to Latin America has also stimulated increased interest in regional initiatives throughout Latin America. For example, the five Andean Nations—Bolivia, Colombia, Peru, Ecuador and Venezuela—have signed an accord to lift all barriers to intra-regional trade by 1991, while Brazil, Argentina, Paraguay and Uruguay, have agreed to form the Mercosur common market by the end of 1995. It would be extremely difficult for a group of countries to negotiate with the United States with a high dispersion in their external tariffs. Countries seeking to negotiate as a group with the United States are thus stimulated to agree first on common external rates. Since this process is taking place at a time of liberalization, these common tariffs toward all trading partners are likely to be lower than those currently protecting these economies. Again the benefits beyond the region should be evident.

It remains to be seen, however, if the US will be able to confine its free trade area initiatives to the Western Hemisphere (and Israel). Far more likely will be pressures on the US to extend its invitation to willing Asian and other economies. The result will be an open agreement which will then be readily linked in a global arrangement.

Table 1 : JAPAN AND SOUTHEAST ASIA
Total Exports by Region of Destination

Billions of $ (percentage)	1973	1980	1985	1988
JAPAN AND SOUTHEAST ASIA	19	64	85	160
	30.5%	27.4%	25.8%	28.8%
Western Hemisphere	20	76	134	197
	31.7%	32.5%	40.6%	35.5%
Western Europe	11	45	48	109
	17.5%	19.2%	14.5%	19.6%
Other (Africa, Middle East, South Asia)	13	49	63	91
	20.3%	20.9%	19.1%	16.3%
TOTAL	63	234	330	557

Source: General Agreement on Tariffs and Trade, *International Trade 1988-89*, volume II.
Figures for Southeast Asia from IMF, *Direction of Trade*, various issues.

Note: WESTERN HEMISPHERE is composed of the USA, Canada, and all of Latin America.
SOUTHEAST ASIA is composed of Korea, Taiwan, Hong Kong, Singapore, Malaysia, Thailand, Indonesia, and the Philippines.
WESTERN EUROPE is composed of the EC plus EFTA.

The Asian bloc allegedly emerging around Japan is the least likely to develop into a formal protectionist arrangement. This region is particularly dependent on extra-regional trade (see Table 1). To be sure, Japan's influence in the East Asian area is likely to increase, but precisely because other Asian nationals are reluctant to submit to an arrangement with a single dominant economy, progress toward a single regional arrangement centred solely on Japan is likely to be slow. Moreover, the US will be unwilling to concede Asia to Japan and is likely to use its influence to prevent a formal Pacific arrangement from which it is excluded. For a time, the US could well be caught in the hypocritical position of promoting Western Hemisphere integration while resisting an Asian arrangement. Eventually, therefore, it will be forced to extend its invitation to form FTAs to willing Asian nations.

Importance of Extra-Bloc Trade. Current trade patterns and trends suggest that extra-bloc trade is vital for each of the current or prospective regional arrangements. While each of the major players may benefit from regional arrangements none can afford to ignore its extra-regional relations. The US, Europe and Japan are all global rather than regional traders.

Tables 1 through 3 provide trade data for three major regions and Japan for selected years from 1973 through 1988. Each of the tables breaks down both the total dollar volume and percentage of exports sold from a specific region to other countries within the same region as well as to nations in other major regions around the world.

Taken together, the tables on trade illustrate the importance of extra-regional trade as a share of total trade. Over half of the Western

Table 2 : WESTERN HEMISPHERE Total Exports by Region of Destination

Billions of $ (percentage)	1973	1980	1985	1988
WESTERN HEMISPHERE	61	189	222	269
	47.3%	46.7%	52.7%	48.1%
Japan and Southeast Asia	18	54	60	103
	14.0%	13.3%	14.3%	18.4%
Western Europe	35	105	85	119
	27.1%	25.9%	20.2%	21.3%
Other (Africa, Middle East, South Asia)	15	57	54	68
	11.6%	14.1%	12.8%	12.2%
TOTAL	129	405	421	559

Source: General Agreement on Tariffs and Trade, 'International Trade 1988-89', volume I. Figures for Southeast Asia from IMF, Direction of Trade, various issues.

Note: WESTERN HEMISPHERE is composed of the USA, Canada, and all of Latin America.
SOUTHEAST ASIA is composed of Korea, Taiwan, Hong Kong, Singapore, Malaysia, Thailand, Indonesia, and the Philippines.
WESTERN EUROPE is composed of the EC plus EFTA.

Table 3 : WESTERN EUROPEAN Total Exports by Region of Destination

Billions of $ (percentage)	1973	1980	1985	1988
WESTERN EUROPE	178 68.5%	551 67.5%	508 65.2%	904 71.3%
Western Hemisphere	31 11.9%	75 9.2%	101 13.0%	137 10.8%
Japan and Southeast Asia	10 3.7%	30 3.7%	34 4.4%	69 5.4%
Other (Africa, Middle East, South Asia)	42 16.0%	160 19.6%	136 17.5%	158 12.5%
TOTAL	260	816	779	1268

Source: General Agreement on Tariffs and Trade, *International Trade 1988-89*, volume II.
Figures for Southeast Asia from IMF, *Direction of Trade*, various issues.

Note: WESTERN HEMISPHERE is composed of the USA, Canada, and all of Latin America.
SOUTHEAST ASIA is composed of Korea, Taiwan, Hong Kong, Singapore, Malaysia, Thailand, Indonesia, and the Philippines.
WESTERN EUROPE is composed of the EC plus EFTA.

Hemisphere's exports and two thirds of Asian exports are outside these regions. Only for Europe are extra-regional exports less than a third of trade. But the share of intra-regional trade in total trade is not the most relevant measure of dependence on extra-regional trade. The importance of extra-regional trade is more usefully measured by the ratio of total extra-regional trade—exports plus imports—to GNP. Table 4 reports these ratios for major trading regions. The table illustrates that measured as a share of GDP, extra-regional trade is actually more important to Europe than to North America. Nonetheless, extra-regional trade remains very significant to North America and to the United States in particular. Since goods are roughly 45 per cent of North American GNP, this implies that about 25 per cent of all American transactions in goods involve an extra-regional buyer or seller. Clearly, efforts to liberalize at the global level through the GATT remain of vital importance.

Table 4 : Extra-regional Trade as Percent of GDP in 1987

All figures in billions of $ Region	GDP	total trade	extra-regional trade	as % of total trade	as % of GDP
North America	4910	815	560	68.7%	11.4%
Western Hemisphere	5675	1025	665	64.9%	11.7%
Japan and Southeast Asia (l)	2910	960	635	66.1%	21.8%
Western Europe	4925	2245	640	28.5%	13.0%

Sources: GDP figures from *GATT International Trade*, 88-89 for the Western Hemisphere and Europe. GDP figures for Japan and Southeast Asia from IMF, IFS Annual 1989.
Total trade from *GATT International Trade*, 87-88 for Western Hemisphere and Europe. Total trade for Asia from IFS, DOT Annual 1989.

Notes: See Table 1 for country groupings.
Total trade equals exports plus imports.

(l) Japan and Southeast Asia figures for 1988.

Tables 1 through 3 also suggest there have not been strong long-run trends towards increased reliance on intra-regional trade. While the share of intra-regional exports in total exports of each region has fluctuated, overall the shares in 1988 for each region were not much different from their levels in 1973.

In sum, the importance of extra-regional trade to nations all over the world means that no region is in a position to sever, or even significantly curtail, its trade ties with the rest of the world by forming closed blocs. While nations have been known to take steps that were against their long term interests, it is clear that each region retains a major interest in the global system. The data thus confirm the importance of extra-regional trade for individual firms in the selling and buying of merchandise.

Motivation. The forces driving nations into regional arrangements are dramatically different from those that drove them into preferential trading blocs in the interwar period. The motive for completing the internal market is not to secure the European market for European producers by providing them preferential access, but instead to facilitate the free movement of goods, services, labour and capital throughout the Community. The EC Single Market initiative reflects the recognition that as the European economies became increasingly integrated, it was necessary to move beyond simply removing border barriers to achieve a much deeper degree of integration. To be sure, there is the hope that a larger market will improve European efficiency, but enhanced competition is precisely the mechanism by which the gains from trade are achieved.

Moreover deeper integration within Europe will facilitate trade with the rest of the world. A common set of standards, for example, makes it easier for *all* who wish to sell in Europe—not just insiders. A tough set of rules which inhibits governments from subsidizing domestic firms aids all their competitors, not only those located in the European Community. Once the larger European economies are committed to allow the free flow of resources within Europe, they will no longer be able to ensure each has a national champion in every industry, located within its territories. This undermining of the nationalist sentiments which drives much of the protectionism in the larger European countries will benefit outsiders. In addition, some of the mechanisms developed by the EC to deal with national diversity could serve as a model for further integration between the EC and its trading partners.

Similarly, the US-Canada free trade agreement was motivated by concerns beyond those relating simply to tariff barriers to merchandise trade. Canada in particular sought protection from the exercise of US trade laws relating to unfair trade. The United States was concerned about Canadian inhibitions on foreign investment. The agreement was wide-ranging, therefore, and included liberalization in services and a bi-national dispute settlement mechanism which again could serve as a model in other integration arrangements. Moreover, there are plans to extend the agreement in the future to deal with discipline on domestic subsidies. Once Canadian subsidies are disciplined, the benefits will accrue to all its trading partners.

Likewise, Mexico is not seeking an FTA with the United States to avoid liberalization with the rest of the world. On the contrary, since the mid-1980s, Mexico has engaged in an extensive unilateral reduction in external restrictions accompanied by internal liberalization. Moreover, in most sectors, tariff barriers against Mexican products entering the US are relatively low. Instead, much of the appeal of an FTA is that it provides credibility and permanence to Mexico's liberalization measures. A second rationale is that an export-oriented Mexico requires secure access to its major trading partner. The FTA is thus an important complement to an outward-oriented policy which is based on attracting foreign investment.

It is ironic that as developing countries have increasingly shifted toward more liberal trading regimes, the differential treatment accorded them by the GATT has actually become a hindrance rather than a benefit. A major motive behind liberalization has been the attraction of foreign capital. However, pledges to maintain open markets made at the GATT have not been particularly credible, in part because of the weakness of the disciplines imposed on developing countries. By contrast, commitments in regional FTAs with developed countries are likely to be much more credible. The GATT dispute settlement mechanism may be weak, but no one doubts the ability of the lawyers in Washington to enforce agreements.

The key point here is that once Mexico accepts obligations *vis-à-vis* the United States to permit foreign investment, to enforce intellectual property rights, to unwind its elaborate protectionist programs for automobiles and electronics, these changes will provide benefits for all its trading partners—not just the United States. US involvement in particular would dramatically enhance the credibility of intra-Latin American regional liberalization arrangements by making the costs of violating the agreement for any individual Latin American country particularly high.

Again the context and motivation for these efforts in Latin America must be appreciated. Over the past three years, in addition to Mexico, Brazil, Argentina and Colombia have all significantly reduced tariff levels as well as the dispersion of tariff levels, while Chilean liberalization has been in place even longer. It is no surprise that the earlier Latin American regional initiatives were failures, since they were implemented in the context of import-substitution policies. The aim of governments with interventionist philosophies was to achieve scale economies in protected regional markets. But these protectionist motives precluded success. However, the current policies are different. They are being implemented by governments proclaiming market-oriented philosophies seeking domestic liberalization and the attraction of foreign capital to service global rather than domestic markets.

To be sure, if these measures are successful, they will increase competition for other nations seeking to attract foreign capital. Pressures will be felt by other countries to avoid being isolated by securing similar arrangements. But as long as the US and the EC offer such nations conditional access to their regional arrangements, this form of competition should be seen as beneficial and liberalizing.

Concluding Comments

This optimistic viewpoint needs to be qualified. While overt protectionist barriers are unlikely, each of the regional arrangements might well resort to more subtle protectionist measures.

In the case of the United States, these typically involve so-called voluntary restraint arrangements (VRAs) and harassment through the use of anti-dumping actions. However, with a Western Hemisphere FTA, Latin American nations would be less susceptible to such measures and in any case have more recourse through special dispute settlement institutions that will inevitably be part of an FTA agreement.

In the case of Europe, protection could be applied through the strict and less-than-transparent application of anti-dumping rules; increased application of safeguard measures; efforts to nurture European firms (through implicit subsidies, selective government procurement and consortia excluding non-European firms); and the promulgation of standards purportedly addressing environmental and safety concerns that have the effect (if not the purpose) of discriminating against extra-bloc trade.

In the case of Asia, protection might be applied through actions taken by Japanese companies, implicitly sanctioned by the Japanese government. It is a commonplace that foreign companies have found the Japanese market hard to crack, largely because of 'hidden barriers' which inhibit them from making sales in Japan.

These concerns highlight the importance of disciplines on these practices at the global level through the GATT. In particular, the Uruguay round contains measures to limit some of these practices. A successful round, which is in the interest of each of the regions, would enhance the prospects that protectionist responses be limited.

Nonetheless, particularly from the standpoint of financial markets, these measures are unlikely to lead to the cataclysmic scenarios resembling the 1930s. Overall, therefore, while progress will undoubtedly not be smooth and linear, the overall direction of the trend toward increased global integration is clear. The key is to appreciate that these deeper degrees of integration cannot necessarily be achieved initially at the global level. Some require much greater and more credible governance than a global institution can provide. Others are acceptable only to particular groups of countries. The correct solution is surely a multi-track approach, with complementary concurrent initiatives proceeding at the global, plurilateral and even bilateral levels. To be sure, there is the danger that this approach will not produce solutions which are completely compatible, but it is surely preferable to restricting progress on integration to the lowest common denominator. If regional arrangements are crafted as open and designed to reinforce rather than resist market forces, they will inevitably become building rather than stumbling blocks in the move towards a more integrated global economy.

Notes and References

1 See Charles Kindleberger, *The World in Depression 1929-1939* (University of California Press, 1986), p. 280.
2 For a discussion of the trading bloc issue, see Andrew Stoeckel, David Pearce and Gary Banks, *Western Trade Blocs: Game Set or Match for Asia-Pacific and the World Economy*, (Canberra, Australia: Centre for International Economics, 1990); Jeffrey J. Schott, ed., *Free Trade Areas and US Trade Policy* (Washington, DC: Institute for International Economics, 1989); and Richard S. Belous and Rebecca S. Hartley, eds., *The Growth of Regional Trading Blocs in the Global Economy* Dornbusch, 'Policy Options for Freer Trade: The Case for Bilateralism' in Robert Z. Lawrence and Charles L. Schultze (eds.), *An American Trade Strategy: Options for the 1990s* (Washington, DC: Brookings Institution, 1991).
3 'The Yen Block', *The Economist*, July 15, 1989, p. 10.
4 See, for example, 'In Asia, the Japanese Hope to Coordinate What Nations Produce', *Wall Street Journal*, August 20, 1990, p. 1.
5 See Paolo Cecchini, *The European Challenge: 1992: The Benefits of a Single Market* (Wildwood House of the Commission of the European Community, 1988) and Richard Baldwin, 'On The Growth Effect Of 1992', *Economic Policy*, 1989, pp. 248-81.
6 See Gary Clyde Hufbauer, 'An Overview', in Hufbauer, ed., *Europe 1992: an American Perspective* (Brookings Institution, 1990), p. 5.

Profit Maximization
and International Competition

SPECIAL MERIT AWARD

Summary

It is argued that the weight of the evidence suggests that large Japanese firms systematically produce and sell more than the standard theory of profit maximization dictates. If this hypothesis is true, several important implications for international trade and competition follow. First, Japanese firms have a natural competitive advantage over Western rivals who maximize profits; the Japanese can survive and even flourish in markets that will not support a competitive rate of return. This edge grows progressively larger in industries on the cutting edge of technology, for faster-growing firms travel down their learning curves faster. Second, the hypothesis can explain why cost increases may not induce Japanese firms to retrench. Third, it may explain why Japanese firms behaved as if they had a cost of capital advantage even when they did not.

Why does not the Darwinian process eliminate firms that fail to maximize profits? I offer three speculative explanations. One is that the Japanese stock market does not discipline non-profit-maximizing managers the way the American stock market does. Another is that growth-oriented firms get more and better work effort from their employees. A third is that technical change proceeds faster in firms that emphasize growth and employee participation. This analysis implies a pessimistic prognosis for US and European firms competing with the Japanese. Japanese companies that are willing to sacrifice profits for growth will outlast their Western rivals in head-to-head competition. If the ultimate structural impediment is not overt trade barriers but the differing goals of the two groups of firms, then market-opening initiatives can only delay the inevitable. If normal business practices in Japan are seen as unfair competition in the West, then trade negotiations are doomed to failure.

Alan S. Blinder is the Gordon S. Rentschler Memorial Professor of Economics at Princeton University. He earned his A.B. at Princeton University (1967), M.Sc. at London School of Economics (1968), and Ph.D. at Massachusetts Institute of Technology (1971)—all in economics. Dr Blinder's fields of research include stabilization policy, macroeconomics, income distribution, and the Japanese economy. He has served as chairman of the Economics Department at Princeton University. He is the founder and director of Princeton's Center for Economic Policy Studies. He served briefly as Deputy Assistant Director of the Congressional Budget Office when that agency started in 1975 and testifies regularly before Congress on a wide variety of public policy issues. The author or co-author of ten books and scores of scholarly articles, he is best known to the public for his lively monthly columns in *Business Week*. His writings have also appeared frequently in *The Washington Post*, *The Boston Globe*, *Newsday*, and other newspapers.

3
Profit Maximization
and International Competition

ALAN S. BLINDER*

This is an essay in persuasion. I advance an unconventional hypothesis which, if true, sheds much light on the seemingly endless trade frictions between Japan and several Western nations, notably the United States. The hypothesis itself is not beyond question and needs to be researched further. But, if it is true, it helps explain not only why Japanese businesses often outcompete their foreign rivals, but also why trade negotiations between the US and Japan consistently produce such meagre results. The hypothesis is simply that large Japanese firms engaged in international trade do not seek to maximize profits. Rather, their drive for growth leads them systematically to produce and sell more than the conventional theory of profit maximization dictates.

My argument proceeds in three steps. First, I marshal evidence against the standard assumption that Japanese firms maximize profits. While the evidence offered in Section I is largely and admittedly anecdotal, there is a fair amount of it; and, as George Stigler once quipped, data is the plural of anecdote. Besides, there is virtually no evidence at all on the other side of the debate, just faith in the postulates of neoclassical economic theory.

The second step is to draw out the implications of this hypothesis for international competition and trade. Details are left to Section II, but the basic idea is quite simple. Suppose Western and Japanese firms face identical cost and demand conditions, but Western firms maximize profits while Japanese firms systematically produce more.[1] Then Japanese companies will sell their wares at lower prices and take markets away from their Western rivals. From the European or American perspective, this behaviour may look like predatory pricing. But to the

* I am grateful to Yukiko Abe, Avinash Dixit, Gene Grossman, and Peter Kenen for helpful comments. The opinions expressed here are, however, entirely my own.

Japanese it will simply be normal business practice—which is one reason why the two sides often talk past each other.

The third step is to address the Darwinian argument for profit maximization. According to conventional economic theory, firms that fail to maximize profits will be driven out of business by the forces of competitive capitalism. The usual argument is that non-profit-maximizing firms will fail to attract new capital and will therefore wither and die. Section III offers several conjectures about why this argument might not apply in Japan.

Before proceeding further, I must issue two important disclaimers. First, it is not my contention that non-profit-maximizing behaviour is the only factor underlying Japan's remarkable export success. Indeed, Alan Krueger and I have suggested elsewhere that Japanese businesses reap substantial efficiency gains from their labour relations practices, practices that Western firms might do well to emulate.[2] Second, I do not claim that nonprofit-maximizing behaviour is the only reason why the Japanese market is hard to penetrate. It may be true that the Japanese erect significant trade barriers to protect their home market, but my thesis is more fundamental. The claim is that, because they care more about growth and less about profits, Japanese businesses have an inherent advantage in international competition. Even on a fully level playing field, profit-maximizing Western firms would still be outcompeted by growth-oriented Japanese firms in many industries.

I. The Goals of the Japanese Firm

Many observers have noted that Japanese and American companies behave differently. The hypothesis that Japanese companies *(kaisha)* routinely produce more output than would maximize profits is one way to interpret and give structure to these differences.

Sometimes it is said that American firms maximize 'short-run profits' while Japanese firms maximize 'long-run profits'. That is not my hypothesis here. The stock market presumably capitalizes long-run (expected) profits into share prices. If the market values companies correctly, American managers striving to maximize stock-market value will be led by a highly visible hand to maximize *long-run* profits. If they fail to do so, either they or the stock market must be making mistakes.

Mistakes happen; but my claim goes deeper and is more basic. It is that there is a systematic difference between the goals of Japanese and Western firms. Specifically, the claim is that managers of large enterprises are willing to sacrifice some of their firms' potential profits to ensure faster growth. The hypothesis is not just that the Japanese are willing to invest today for future returns; all but the most myopic managers will do that. It is that they are willing to sacrifice profits indefinitely for the sake of greater size.

To those schooled in conventional economic theory, this may seem an outlandish notion. But two types of evidence support it. One is that much of the behaviour of Japanese firms looks puzzling when viewed through the prism of profit maximization. The other is that few students of the Japanese system believe that the *kaisha* maximize profits. I take these up in turn.

Japanese companies appear to be much more adept at growing fast and gaining market share than at generating profits. As Clyde Prestowitz, Jr. puts it: 'The Japanese are not averse to making money; all things being equal, they'd like to make more. But if the choice is between growth and profit, it will be growth every time'.[3] Similarly, business consultants James Abegglen and George Stalk write of 'the strong bias toward growth of the successful *kaisha*'.[4] This, I believe, is why Japanese firms compete ferociously in markets with profit margins so thin that American firms find the prospects daunting. Here are a few examples:

– In an often-cited survey of Japanese and US companies conducted by Japan's Economic Planning Agency a decade ago, American companies listed return on investment as their principal objective. There was no serious competition; stock-market price was a distant second and market share finished third.[5] Japanese companies, by contrast, put market share first, return on investment second, and introducing new products third. Very few even listed stock-market price among their top ten objectives.[6]

– In *Business Week*'s latest list of the largest companies in the world, all of the top five, and six of the top ten firms, ranked by *sales* were Japanese. But only one of the top ten companies ranked by *profits* was Japanese; Toyota at rank 7.[7] Is this because the Japanese maximize long-run rather than short-run profits? I doubt it. Giants like Toyota, Mitsui, and Mitsubishi are old enough so that they should now be realizing their long-run profit potential.

- Between 1979 and 1986, Nippon Electric Company (NEC) grew much faster than its American rival, Motorola, and greatly increased its market share. Yet, during those years, Motorola's return on assets ranged between 9.4% and 16% while NEC's ranged between 4% and 7%.[8] Although Motorola was the more profitable company, it is now dwarfed by its Japanese competitor.

- A former NEC executive told Prestowitz that Japanese managers, who typically come from engineering backgrounds, do not worry about capital costs. The executive claimed that he had never seen a discounted cash flow analysis in all his years at NEC.[9] Can such a firm be maximizing profits?

- Sony's Akio Morita once told a prominent American CEO that Sony simply had to be at the technological frontier at all times.[10] When the American related this story (approvingly) to me, the neoclassical economist in me almost blurted out: 'But that can't be profit maximizing behaviour!' It is probably not; but that is precisely the point.

Most experienced observers of the Japanese system have concluded that Japanese firms maximize something other than profits. As I have noted, Abegglen and Stalk emphasize growth. Ryutaro Komiya, a leading academic economist now associated with MITI, believes that Japanese firms maximize the welfare of their employees.[11] Masahiko Aoki, perhaps the premier theorist of the Japanese system, modifies this somewhat to argue that Japanese managers mediate between workers and shareholders by maximizing a weighted average of profits and employee welfare. He concludes that the Japanese firm 'pursues a higher growth rate than the level that short-run share price maximization would warrant to deliver extra benefit to the quasi-permanent employee'.[12]

Journalist Karel van Wolferen, in his scholarly tome on the Japanese power structure, writes that: 'Whereas in the West . . . economic factors such as profitability determine a company's success, in Japan success is measured more by political indicators: the company's size and market share'. He notes that, 'The emphasis on conquering market shares and *the ability to do so at the expense of profits* are relatively new [emphasis added]'.[13] Douglas Kenrick, a New Zealander who has run his own business in Japan for more than 40 years, writes that the 'feeling that the place-of-work, the corporation, exists for the employees and to give a service to its customers, not the shareholders, is taken for granted'.[14] Most of the Japanese businessmen, government officials and economists I interviewed in the summer of 1991 thought that employee welfare, more than profits, motivates the Japanese firm.

Impressions all, to be sure. But virtually no evidence stands on the other side.

If not profit maximization, then what is the objective of the Japanese firm? I have culled four main alternative goals from the scholarly and popular literature. It is a fascinating and worthwhile intellectual exercise to seek evidence on which is more important. But, for present purposes, it does not much matter since each leads to the same conclusion: that the Japanese firm produces beyond the profit-maximizing level.

1. *Maximizing growth*: Abegglen and Stalk and many others emphasize growth in sales an hypothesis first advanced (for large American firms!) by William Baumol more than 30 years ago.[15] It is symptomatic that Toyota, already the most profitable company in Japan, has stated that its long-term goal is to be the world's *biggest* automobile maker, not the most profitable.

2. *Maximizing market share*: This goal differs from the first only under unusual circumstances. For example, suppose a multinational corporation supplies different markets from independently operated production facilities. Then it is logically possible that maximizing market share in each country might not maximize overall corporate growth. But this is splitting hairs; for the most part, growing and increasing market share amount to the same thing.

3. *Maximizing employee welfare*: Komiya's hypothesis that the *kaisha* are run for the benefit of their employees seems at first to be quite different from growth maximization. But Aoki points out that the two goals normally coincide under the Japanese lifetime employment system. The reason is that Japanese employees make careers within a single firm, prospering as they move up the corporate ladder. A rapidly-growing firm offers its workers much greater opportunities for promotion.[16]

4. *'Collecting trophies'*: This goal does not appear in the theoretical literature, but it seems to capture salient aspects of Japanese business behaviour. One case in point is Morita's attitude that Sony must always be on the technological frontier. Another is the Japanese penchant for acquiring prominent properties like Rockefeller Center or the Pebble Beach golf club at inflated prices. Mitsui Real Estate's man in New York told writer Michael Lewis that no Japanese investor has yet made money in the New York real estate market. What, then, motivated all

42   *Alan S. Blinder*

those purchases? According to Lewis, it was the drive for status back in Japan. When Mitsubishi Estates outbid Mitsui for a 51% interest in Rockefeller Center, 'it wasn't a normal American-style corporate rivalry. It had nothing to do with who made the most money. It had to do with the prestige of the company, with being the biggest'.[17] In the process, Mitsubishi paid what industry professionals believe to be roughly double the property's value.

Notice that these four goals normally coincide rather than conflict. Acquiring major prizes for the corporate trophy case generally increases sales and market share and creates more opportunities for employees. On the other hand, all four normally conflict with profit maximization. For this reason, I will be deliberately vague hereafter in referring to 'size maximization' as the goal of the Japanese firm.

II. Some Implications for Competition and Trade

Let us suppose, then, that Japanese firms maximize size rather than profits. What are the implications for international trade and competition?

– The first implication is obvious: The *kaisha* will be eager to sell more goods at lower prices than their profit-maximizing rivals. So Japanese firms will enter markets that Western firms shun; and they will cling to market share even when Western firms are exiting due to low profitability.[18] This difference gives the Japanese a natural edge in head to head competition: they can succeed by their criterion (that is, grow larger) while Western firms are failing by theirs (that is, not earning a competitive rate of return). Beleaguered Western firms will naturally view such competition as unfair. The Japanese are, after all, selling below full cost—including an appropriate return on capital. The Japanese, who are just practising business as usual, will find the charge perplexing.

– Size maximizers have an even sharper advantage in technologically progressive industries with important learning curves, precisely the areas in which Japanese industry has succeeded so well of late. To see why, imagine that a Western profit maximizer is competing with a Japanese firm which always produces more under the same cost and demand conditions. The Japanese firm will ride down its learning curve faster. Hence, even if it starts the competitive race with no cost advantage, it will soon acquire one. Once this cost advantage has emerged, the profit maximizer is in deep trouble. While it understands the long-run advantages of learning by doing, it finds it unprofitable to learn as fast as the revenue maximizer. The latter not only produces more at any given level of marginal cost, but also reduces its marginal cost faster. So the profit maximizing tortoise never catches the size maximizing hare.

– A third implication follows when market conditions are favourable enough to let Japanese firms, at the margin, ignore profits entirely. For example, suppose the Japanese firm maximizes revenue subject to a minimum-profit constraint that is not binding. Then the *kaisha* becomes a pure revenue maximizer and its production and price decisions are entirely decoupled from production costs. If costs increase— say, because of OPEC or currency realignments—a pure revenue maximizer will sacrifice profit rather than scale back its operations. A profit maximizer will contract.

– A size maximizer will also act *as if* it has a lower cost of capital than its profit maximizing rivals: It will invest more at all margins. Why is that? Simply because a size maximizing firm will appraise investment opportunities by their contributions to, say, the firm's *growth*, not their contributions to *profit*. If the cost of capital in the US and Japan is, for example, 10%, an American firm will reject a project returning 9%; but a Japanese firm may accept it.

Japan's cost of capital advantage has received much attention of late in academia and in the business press.[19] This advantage seems to have existed for more than a decade, and is the leading explanation for why Japanese firms invest more than American firms. But a simple fact seems to have been lost in the debate. From the time of its postwar 'take-off' in the mid-1950s until sometime in the early 1970s, Japan had no capital-cost advantage over the United States. Yet that is precisely when the Japanese formulated and carried out their high-investment strategy.

We therefore have two competing theories of why Japanese firms invest more than American firms: (1) the cost of capital is lower in Japan, or (2) Japanese firms value size *per se*. Normally, these two theories yield identical predictions about investment behaviour. But current events may provide an unusually decisive test. In the last year or two, rising interest rates and falling stock prices in Japan, coupled with falling interest rates and rising stock prices in the US, have essentially eliminated Japan's cost of capital advantage. If the cost of capital differential was the main reason for Japan's higher investment rates, the Japanese should no longer invest more than the Americans. If size-maximizing behaviour was the reason, the investment gap should remain.

– A final implication follows from the hypothesis that the Japanese view bigger as better. A firm that is more concerned with size than profits will be eager to acquire assets. It will therefore systematically 'overpay' for properties—*if* these properties are valued according to the discounted present value calculations relevant to profit maximization. This seems to be precisely how American business people characterize Japanese purchases. Whether it is Hawaiian hotels, New York skyscrapers, or interests in investment firms, American observers always seem to claim that the Japanese overpay for the assets they buy. That is, of course, why the Americans sell so eagerly.

III. Survival of the Fittest?

The notion that firms do not maximize profits surfaces regularly in the economic literature, where it is normally dismissed with the following Darwinian argument. Firms that fail to maximize profits will generate smaller returns for the capitalists who own them. Their stock market values will fall, making them vulnerable to takeovers and/or unable to raise funds in a competitive capital market. Eventually, they will perish or be swallowed up by profit maximizers. Why does this argument not hold in Japan? I cannot give a definitive answer, but offer three speculative hypotheses.[20]

The first is that the Japanese stock market does not discipline non-profit maximizing managers the way the US stock market does. For one thing, it is well known that much of the equity in Japanese companies is locked up in cross-holdings. For example, a 1988 MITI survey estimated that almost 80% of the shares on the Tokyo stock exchange were held by 'relationship-oriented' investors, e.g. lenders and associated corporations.[21] This reduces selling pressure and all but immunizes non-profit maximizing managers from takeover bids. But it is not a sufficient explanation, for the docile behaviour of arms-length investors still needs to be explained. Stock prices are, after all, determined at the margin. Why do profit-driven investors not punish managers with low share prices?

Perhaps they do; the shares of Mitsubishi Estates, for example, have dropped relative to the Nikkei index since its purchase of Rockefeller

Center. However, Japanese managers can ignore stock market values in a way that, say, US managers cannot. Arms-length shareholders in Japan are essentially rentiers with little or no influence on corporate behaviour.

The second hypothesis, which is equally speculative, has to do with a possible shortcoming of standard economic thought. Neoclassical trade theory, like microeconomic theory in general, assumes that each firm has a technologically determined production function that tells it how much output it will get from any given amounts of capital, labour, and material inputs. According to theory, firms hire labour and other inputs, put them to work, and get the output specified by the production function. Workers have neither authority nor discretion over what they do.

But suppose labour is not so passive as this. Suppose workers need to be properly motivated to put forth their best efforts, as assumed in some versions of efficiency wage theory. Conventional profit maximization, which assigns all marginal returns to the capitalists, gives workers only weak incentives to perform up to their abilities. A system that features higher wages, greater job security, and more employee involvement may provide much stronger incentives. If so, the production function of a firm following 'Japanese' practices might be superior to that of a conventional profit maximizer. In that case, the Darwinian struggle might not eliminate the size maximizers.[22]

The accompanying figure illustrates. Assume for concreteness that the Japanese firm maximizes sales subject to a profit constraint indicated by the horizontal line at C. In both panels, the lower profit hill shows the possibilities available to a conventional profit maximizer, its best choice is clearly point M. The higher profit hill shows the superior

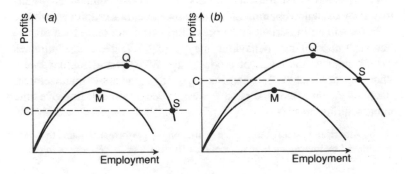

possibilities presumed available to the sales maximizing firm. The key idea is that the technology is linked to the firm's behaviour. By choosing point S, the sales maximizing firm sacrifices some profits. But, by adopting the behaviour that goes along with this choice, it reaps productivity gains because its employees work harder and smarter.

Superficially, point Q would appear to be a better choice than S, for it leads to more profit. But the hypothesis is that point Q is an illusion; if the firm changes to profit maximizing behaviour, its employees will perform less well, leaving it with only the inferior profit hill and point M as its best choice. In panel (a), this change would raise profits, so that standard Darwinian argument holds. Profit maximizing behaviour dominates sales maximizing behaviour. In panel (b), however, the efficiency gains from sales maximizing behaviour are so large that point S is actually more profitable than point M. A sales maximizer actually makes more profit than a firm that sets out to maximize profits in the usual way (i.e., by equating marginal revenue to marginal cost). This means, of course, that point S, not point M, is the true profit-maximizing solution.

To draw something does not make it true. But there is intriguing evidence that profit sharing, which helps align the interests of capital and labour, raises labour productivity.[23] And there are also dramatic examples, like the NUMMI plant in Fremont, California, where Japanese management techniques have led to drastic improvements in output from almost the same capital and labour inputs.

This relative efficiency argument becomes potentially much more powerful when we move from statics to dynamics. For one thing, a more efficient labour force presumably raises the rate of return on capital, thereby encouraging more investment which, in turn, raises the productivity of labour. A nice sort of virtuous circle. In a similar vein, Aoki argues that incumbent workers in Japanese companies prefer growth by capital deepening rather than by expanding employment.[24]

Perhaps more important is the possibility—it is not more than that—that size maximizing behaviour may actually increase *the rate of growth*, not just the level, of productivity. Why? Haruo Shimada and other Japanese labour economists argue that Japanese management practices encourage workers to *kaizen*, or continuously improve the manufacturing process.

. . . the American system . . . places a ceiling on the performance gains that can be achieved by improving human resource effectiveness—a ceiling not in place in the Japanese system. Japanese companies emphasize human resource effectiveness because it is a technological imperative to achieve continued gains in performance (emphasis added).[25]

If Shimada is right, then a firm that maximizes sales or employee welfare rather than profits might enjoy a faster pace of technological improvement than a conventional profit maximizer. Once again, Darwinian forces will work in its favour rather than against it.

IV. Recapitulation

The argument can be summarized briefly. A substantial amount of anecdotal evidence suggests that large Japanese firms systematically produce and sell more than the standard theory of profit maximization dictates. Suppose this hypothesis is true. What follows?

First, Japanese firms have a natural competitive advantage over Western rivals who maximize profits; the *kaisha* can flourish (by their own standards) even in markets that will not support a competitive rate of return. This edge grows progressively larger in industries on the cutting edge of technology, where learning curves are important. Second, the hypothesis can explain why cost increases may not induce Japanese firms to retrench. Third, it may explain why Japanese firms behaved as if they had a cost of capital advantage even when they did not.

But why does the Darwinian process not eliminate firms that fail to maximize profits? Here the argument is on shakier grounds, but I offer three speculative explanations. One is that the Japanese stock market does not effectively discipline non-profit maximizing managers in the way the American stock market does. Another is that size maximizing firms get more and better work effort from their employees. A third is that technical change proceeds faster in a size maximizing environment with employee participation.

One important caveat must be entered at this point: The aforementioned arguments cannot apply to the entire Japanese economy. For one thing, Japan, like any nation, must reckon with resource constraints that make it impossible to produce more of *every* commodity. If some Japanese industries are bigger than they would be under profit maximization, then other industries must be smaller. For another, extreme export success in some industries will raise the value of the yen, thereby handicapping other export (and import-competing) industries.

Where, then, does the model apply? Clearly not to small firms nor perhaps even to large firms controlled by owner-managers. Rather, the model applies mainly to large firms in which management enjoys considerable autonomy, especially in technologically-progressive industries with steep learning curves. Here, the model predicts, is where Japan will be most competitive on world markets.

What, then, are the implications for international trade? Not very good for the United States and Europe, I am afraid. If major Japanese companies are willing systematically to sacrifice profits for growth, they will outlast their Western rivals in head-to-head competition—as has recently happened in semiconductors. If the ultimate 'structural impediment' is not overt trade barriers but the differing goals of the two groups of firms, then market-opening initiatives can only delay the inevitable triumph of the *kaisha*. If normal business practices in Japan are perceived as unfair competition in the West, then trade negotiations are doomed to failure. After all, what right do Americans have to demand that Japan change its eminently successful ways?

There is, however, one possibly cheerful resolution. If the Japanese practices that I have characterized as size maximization really amount to a more sophisticated way to maximize profits (as is the case in panel (b) of the figure, for example), then Western firms may be expected to catch on. That is one reason why more Western understanding of the Japanese system is so important.

Notes

1 The crucial point is not that Western firms literally maximize profits but only that Japanese firms will produce more under the same circumstances.
2 Alan S. Blinder and Alan B. Krueger, 'International Differences in Labour Turnover: A Comparative Study with Emphasis on the US and Japan', mimeo, April 1991. It was in the context of researching this paper that I became convinced that large Japanese firms do not maximize profits.
3 Clyde V. Prestowitz, Jr., *Trading Places* (New York: Basic Books), 1989, p. 311.
4 James C. Abegglen and George Stalk, Jr., *Kaisha: The Japanese Corporation* (New York: Basic Books), 1985, p. 6.
5 I interpret return on investment and stock market value as more or less the same thing, and both as connoting profit-maximizing behaviour.

6 Cited in Abegglen and Stalk, op. cit., page 177.

7 *Business Week*, July 15, 1991, p. 52.

8 Prestowitz op. cit., p. 362.

9 Ibid., p. 311.

10 I subsequently verified this directly with Morita.

11 Ryutaro Komiya, 'Japanese Firms, Chinese Firms: Problems for Economic Reform in China', I, *Journal of the Japanese and International Economies*, March 1987, pp. 31-61.

12 Masahiko Aoki, *Information Incentives, and Bargaining in the Japanese Economy* (Cambridge, UK: Cambridge University Press), 1988, page 165.

13 Karel van Wolferen, *The Enigma of Japanese Power* (New York: Knopf), 1989, pages 172, 396.

14 Douglas Moore Kenrick, *The Success of Competitive-Communism in Japan* (London: Macmillan), 1988, page 8. In fairness, it should be mentioned that, somewhat contradictorily, Kenrick emphasizes the Japanese firm's drive for profits.

15 William J. Baumol, *Business Behaviour, Value and Growth* (New York: Macmillan), 1959.

16 In Aoki's model, workers wish to maximize a function of the wage bill and the growth rate; the latter enters the objective function owing to prospects for promotion. See Aoki, op. cit., page 193.

17 Michael Lewis, *Pacific Rift* (Whittle Direct Books, 1991), pages 67, 75. The quotation comes from a real estate specialist.

18 Baldwin and Krugman, Dixit and others have recently offered a 'hysteresis' explanation for why the Japanese may remain in an unprofitable market once they have entered it. The argument, based as it is on fixed costs and *profit* maximization, applies equally well to Western firms. My hypothesis is different and implies an asymmetry in behaviour between the two types of firms. But it in no way contradicts or denies the point made by Baldwin-Krugman and Dixit. See Richard Baldwin and Paul Krugman, 'Persistent Trade Effects of Large Exchange Rate Shocks', *Quarterly Journal of Economics*, Vol. 54, November 1989, pp. 635–654 and Avinash Dixit, 'Hysteresis, Import Penetration, and Exchange Rate Pass-Through', *Quarterly Journal of Economics*, Vol. 54, May 1989, pp. 205–228.

19 For a recent survey see James Poterba, 'Comparing the Cost of Capital in the United States and Japan: A Survey of Methods', *Federal Reserve Bank of New York Quarterly Review*, Vol. 15, No. 3–4, Winter 1991, pp. 20–32.

20 There is a fourth hypothesis: that the Japanese government saves firms from oblivion by rigging the deck in their favour—for example, by protecting and cartelizing the domestic market so that high profits at home compensate for low profits abroad. I ignore this possibility here because my objective is to examine the hypothesis that Japanese firms would enjoy an advantage in international trade *even in the absence of all trade barriers*.

50   *Alan S. Blinder*

21 Cited in Burton G. Malkiel, 'The Influence of Conditions in Financial Markets on the Time Horizons of Business Managers: An International Comparison', CEPS Working Paper No. 2, Princeton University, March 1991.

22 Fershtman and Judd have provided a game-theoretic argument for why profit-maximizing owners might, under some circumstances, give managers incentives to maximize sales. See Chaim Fershtman and Kenneth L. Judd, 'Equilibrium Incentives in Oligopoly', *American Economic Review*, Vol. 77, No. 5 (December 1987), pp. 927-940.

23 Alan S. Blinder (ed.), *Paying for Productivity: A Look at the Evidence* (Washington, DC: Brookings), 1990.

24 Aoki, op. cit., page 168.

25 H. Shimada, 'Japanese Management of Auto Production in the United States: An Overview of "Humanwear Technology"', in K Yamamura (ed.), *Japanese Investment in the United States: Should We Be Concerned?*, (Society for Japanese Studies), 1989, p. 193.

Einigkeit Macht Stark—
The Deutsche Mark Also?

THIRD PRIZE

Summary

The dominant view among academics and policy-makers is that German unification requires, and will lead to, a real appreciation of the deutsche mark. The main argument advanced for this view is that higher demand in the ex-GDR increases demand for West German goods and thereby pushes up their price.

So far, the deutsche mark has not appreciated in real terms. The slight depreciation since unification also squares with intuition: would anybody expect the US dollar to appreciate if the US absorbed Mexico?

We argue that economic theory properly applied does not generate the conclusion that a real appreciation is required. The key point is that goods which are non-tradable between, say, West Germany and France are also non-tradable with the ex-GDR. Intra-German transfers lower real income in West Germany and thereby the demand for West German non-tradable goods. The real exchange rate of the deutsche mark, say against the French franc, should therefore depreciate.

Increased import demand in united Germany is mainly due to a shift in demand away from home goods in the ex-GDR and towards 'western' goods, including apparently a high proportion of goods not produced in West Germany. This 'unification effect' is confirmed by a simulation of import demand and accounts for the reduction in the trade surplus of Germany. A real appreciation is not required to achieve this redirection of trade flows.

Daniel Gros is Senior Research Fellow and Director of the financial Markets Unit of the Centre for European Policy Studies (CEPS). An honours graduate of the University of Rome he received his MA from the University of Southern California and his Ph.D. in economics from the University of Chicago. Dr Gros has concentrated his research on issues related to European integration and, more recently, on the transformation process in central Europe and the Soviet Union. He has served as an economist in the Research Department of the International Monetary Fund and as an adviser in Directorate General II of the European Communities.

Alfred Steinherr is Director of the Financial Research Department at the European Investment Bank in Luxembourg. An honours graduate of the University of Lausanne in law and economics, he received an MS in mathematics from George Washington University and a Ph.D. in economics from Cornell University (1973). He joined the Catholic University of Louvain in Belgium in 1973 and was professor of economics there until 1988.

His international experience includes two years as senior economist with the International Monetary Fund in Washington, and three years as economic adviser with the Commission of the European Communities.

4
Einigkeit Macht Stark—
The Deutsche Mark Also?
Unity Means Strength
For the Deutsche Mark as Well?

DANIEL GROS AND ALFRED STEINHERR*

Introduction

In the debate preceding German unification most economists favoured fixed but adjustable or flexible exchange rates to provide East Germany with an additional policy tool for a transition period.[1] For West Germany also, currency union was seen as quite undesirable. With their newly acquired freedom, East Germans were expected to go on a spending spree which, together with the effects of price liberalization, would make control of inflation difficult in united Germany.

The external effect of unification was widely expected to result in a real appreciation of the deutsche mark for several mutually reinforcing reasons. Some identified the increase in aggregate demand in united Germany as a cause of rising prices for non-tradable goods and hence the real exchange rate (Artus (1991), Fitoussi and Phelps (1990)). Others noted that the increase in demand in the ex-GDR would generate excess demand for West German goods and a real appreciation would be required to redirect German exports to domestic uses (Burda (1990) and MacKibbin (1990)). A study by the IMF (1990), saw real appreciation as a consequence of rapid growth paired with expansionary fiscal policy and restrictive monetary policy. And, finally, from a longer-run perspective, it was noted that the capital-labour ratio of united Germany would fall and hence its export potential (Basevi (1990) and Siebert (1991)). Wyplosz (1991) is an

* Opinions expressed in this paper are purely personal and should not be correlated with those, if any, of the authors' institutions.

exception: using an inter-temporal framework he concludes that the real exchange rate change is ambiguous in the short run and a real depreciation is required in the steady state because of the fall in net external assets.

We hold different views about all these conjectures (Gros and Steinherr (1990)). However, currency union is history and the question of whether it was the right decision or not has lost its drama.[2] More interesting, and still highly pertinent today, is the question whether the deutsche mark needs to appreciate in real terms as a consequence of unfication. More generally and more provocatively, would anybody expect the US dollar to appreciate if the United States absorbed Mexico?

Some intuition is provided by asking the hypothetical question whether the deutsche mark would have appreciated (or have been revalued) in real terms within the EMS if the ex-GDR had opted for fixed exchange rates. The two phenomena with an effect on the exchange rate are the shift in the composition of demand in the ex-GDR[3] and the transfer-induced increase in purchasing power (also in the ex-GDR). The real exchange rate of the deutsche mark would only require an appreciation if increased demand for imports in the new *Länder* were biased in favour of West German goods. Even then, given the small size of the GDR and the limited scope for this potential bias, the real appreciation required would be quite small. More importantly, this effect is at least partly offset by the transfer-induced reduction in real income in West Germany, reducing both the demand for tradables and for non-tradables in West Germany.[4] As the price of the latter will need to decrease to clear the market for non-tradables, the deutsche mark's real exchange rate is more likely to depreciate.

Thus, when it is recognized that, first, increased demand in the ex-GDR need not be strongly biased in favour of West German goods and against goods from the rest of the world; and that, second, the only clearly bilateral effect between the two Germanys is the transfer, then the presumption of real appreciation needed for the deutsche mark within the EMS becomes much weaker. This is what most people would have expected in the case where the ex-GDR had retained its own currency.

These results are also of relevance in other Eastern European countries with a fixed exchange rate and one would not expect the deutsche mark to appreciate within the EMS because Yugoslavia has pegged its currency to the deutsche mark and receives transfer payments.

In the following, we refine this analysis and argue that it is still pertinent for currency union. The essential point is that goods which were non-tradable before unification are likely to remain so after unification. It will also be convenient to distinguish between the demand effects that arise in the short run and the supply effects from factor movements that might take longer to materialize.

1. The Short to Medium Run: Demand Effects

Imagine an EMS composed of two countries: France and Germany. Suddenly demand goes up in one country, Germany. Part of this increase in demand falls on tradable goods, thus reducing the external surplus of Germany, while the remainder goes towards non-tradable goods (whose supply is much less elastic than that of tradables) thus requiring an increase in the relative price of German *non-tradables*. At given nominal wages, an increase in the relative price of German non-tradables (*vis-à-vis* French non-tradables) requires then an appreciation of the nominal exchange rate of the deutsche mark. This is the standard framework that has been used to justify the hypothesis that German unification requires a real appreciation of the deutsche mark The crucial point in this line of reasoning is thus that, at given German wages, the exchange rate of the deutsche mark (against, the French franc for example) determines the price of German goods relative to French goods.

This conventional analysis is wrong because it does not take into account that German reunification has had completely different effects in the two parts of Germany. The key is that their real economies are completely different although they use the same currency. In our view it is essential to distinguish between the effects German unification has on the demand for non-tradable goods produced in East and West Germany. The relative price of these two goods can alter through changes in wages in East Germany, relative to those in West Germany.

If the standard tradables/non-tradables model used above is applied to the problem at hand, and if one takes into account the differential impact of unification on West and East Germany, then the conclusion is that no real appreciation of the deutsche mark would be required. A real appreciation of the deutsche mark would be required only if the demand for *West German* non-tradables were to go up. This in turn can happen only if *West Germans* spend more. It is therefore essential to determine whether unification increases the spending of West Germans.

Although overall demand in Germany has gone up there is no reason for demand by West Germans to go up (above trend) since West Germans lend or transfer large amounts of purchasing power to East Germany. On the contrary, West Germans know that they will have to pay sooner or later for most of the debt accumulated by the government to rebuild the ex-GDR. The expectation of higher future taxes is the reason why in general private savings increase if the government deficit rises.[5] Econometric studies in IMF (1990) indicate that in the short run the increase in private savings is not equal to government dissavings, but still about 30% of additional government dissavings is offset by higher private savings. In the long run the offset rises to almost 100%.

There is already some evidence that this is happening, since the savings ratio of private households in West Germany (savings relative to disposable income) has increased from 13.5% in 1989 to 14.8% in 1990. The most recent data shows that there has been no noticeable further change. The private savings rate for the first quarter of 1991 (seasonally unadjusted) is at the same level as the first quarter of 1990 (and, of course, above the first quarter of 1989, see Table 1). This implies that overall demand by West German households cannot be the driving force behind the current boom in West Germany. Without an increase in overall demand by West German households there is no increase in the demand for West German non-tradables and there is therefore also no reason why the relative price of, say French and German, non-tradables should change. Hence, there is no need for a real appreciation of the deutsche mark or a realignment in the EMS.

The increase in the savings rate suggests that the expectations of future taxes are so strong that demand by households in the Western part of Germany actually falls below trend. Part of that decrease in demand would fall on non-tradables requiring a real depreciation of the deutsche mark, which could be achieved through lower German inflation and an unchanged nominal exchange rate.[6] The evidence for this view comes from the fact that inflation in West Germany has not accelerated as much as was expected, and under this hypothesis, it should fall back as household demand in the West is checked. Though German inflation has risen, it has remained below the EMS average, and with nominal exchange rates against the EMS currencies not much changed since 1989, the deutsche mark has depreciated in real terms.

The relative price of East German non-tradables (goods that cannot be traded between say Germany and France can presumably be considered also as non-tradables between East and West Germany) may of course have to change. But that relative price can change easily. Indeed a large jump already occurred through conversion at 1:1 for wages and further adjustments did take place through wage increases in the territory of the GDR.

The behaviour of prices in West Germany up to the end of 1990 fully bears out our analysis. There is no price index of non-tradables, but there is an index for 'services and repairs' which should account for the bulk of non-tradables. The ratio of the index for 'services and repairs' to the overall consumer price index can thus be taken as a crude approximation of the relative price of non-tradables in West Germany. As shown in Table 1 that ratio followed an upwards trend until mid 1990 (bringing it from 100 in 1985 to 105.6 just before unification, productivity gains in services are usually smaller than in the rest of the economy), but it has remained below that value since then. This is further evidence of the view that demand for non-tradables in West Germany has not increased.

Another framework that is often used to argue that German unification requires a real appreciation of the deutsche mark is one in which the emphasis is on nationally differentiated goods that are tradable. In this approach there would also be a need for a real appreciation of the deutsche mark if East Germans (they are the ones who receive the additional purchasing power) have a higher propensity to spend on West German tradables than West Germans. Although East Germans obviously prefer imported, Western goods to their own goods there is no reason why they should prefer goods from West Germany to goods from Japan or France.

The only way to make actual data bear on this question is to use the experience of other European economies of a size comparable to the ex-GDR (e.g. Holland, Belgium). These countries receive only about one fourth of all their imports from the Federal Republic. Applying the same percentage to the new *Länder* implies that even if the new *Länder* run a current account deficit with the Federal Republic of 120 billion deutsche mark per annum (4% of West German GDP) the additional demand for West German exportables would be only about 30 billion deutsche mark (and the reduction in the German current account surplus would be 90 billion deutsche mark).[7] These additional 'exports' of West Germany represent only about 5% of the overall

Table 1: West Germany: data used in text

	1989	1990				1991	
		I	II	III	IV	I	II
in deutsche mark bn (seasonally unadjusted)							
Exports	640	169	159	152	163	161	159
Imports	506	132	131	133	155	156	161
Balance	134	37	28	19	8	54	-2
M1 (growth rate)	5.5	-8.4	17.0	4.1*	16.2*	-9.2*	
M3	5.5	-3.5	15.9	1.3*	5.7*	-2.7*	
Private saving (% of personal income seasonally unadjusted)	13.5	16.8	13.2	12.8	16.3	16.7	
			(average 1990: 14.8)				
Seasonally adjusted	13.5	14.2	15.0	15.3	14.7	4.1	
Prices (all 1985 = 100):							
Overall CPI	105.2	106.3	106.8	107.5	108.1	109.0	110.5
services	109.9	112.5	112.9	112.6	113.2	114.5	116.4
Services/CPI	104.4	105.8	105.6	104.7	104.7	105.0	105.3
Real exchange rate 1972 = 100	92.1	92.3	91.0	90.7	92.3	90.1	87.9

* West and East Germany combined
Source: Deutsche Bundesbank, monthly reports

exports of the Federal Republic of Germany (in 1989, i.e. prior to unification) which total 600 million deutsche mark and their effective supply is not likely to require a large price change. The crude estimates presented in section 3 below confirm this order of magnitude.

2. The Long Run: Factor Movements

A different way to look at the implications of Germany unification for the EMS is to take into account not only its effects on demand, but to use the standard Heckscher-Ohlin framework, based on factor endowments and movements.[8] The crucial point in this framework is that East Germany starts out with a much lower capital-labour ratio. This should lead to capital flows into East Germany and should also be reflected in the capital intensity of the goods traded by East Germany.[9] However, given that the German capital market is open to the rest of the world, most of the capital will come from the rest of the world (hence the lower external surpluses). As long as the East German economy is in the factor price equalization region, movements of goods and factors can equalize prices, and, consequently, there is again no need for a change in the relative price of (West) German exports relative to its imports.

3. The Effects of Unification on Germany's External Accounts

During the first quarter of 1991, Germany's current account went into deficit for the first time since the early 1980s. The German trade account surplus decreased from deutsche mark 37.8 bn for the first quarter of 1990 to a deficit of over deutsche mark 2 bn for the first quarter of 1991. As suggested by our back-of-the-envelope calculations, unification thus had a profound effect on Germany's external accounts even without a real appreciation of the deutsche mark. It is, of course, impossible to determine exactly the source of the increased demand for imports in Germany; but a useful approximation can be obtained with the following procedure which concentrates on merchandise trade only:

i) Estimate the demand for imports of the Federal Republic up to 1989 (explanatory variables: real exchange rate and domestic demand).

ii) Use the estimated coefficients and the available data on the determinants of (West German) imports to forecast the demand for imports up to the present.

iii) Take the difference between the actual and the forecast values for imports and attribute this difference to unification.

The result of this procedure can be seen in Figure 1 which displays the actual values of West German imports and the actual values of total German imports (available only since July 1990) as well as the forecast obtained from a simple import demand equation.[10] This forecast uses actual values of total domestic demand for West Germany and the actual real exchange rate of the deutsche mark.

60   *Daniel Gros and Alfred Steinherr*

Unification has not affected substantially the relative prices faced by
West Germans (within the EMS exchange rates did not change at all,
and the dollar moved down and up without any major net change since
1989). There is therefore no reason why West Germans should change
their spending on imports. The solid line in Figure 1 therefore displays
the import demand one can expect from West Germany. The difference
between the solid line and the actual values can therefore be imputed to
imports going to East Germany, either directly or indirectly via West
Germany. However, since it is irrelevant whether the imports used in
the East go first through West Germany (e.g. through West German
retailers) this distinction is not pursued any further.

Figure 1 The effects of unification on German import demand.

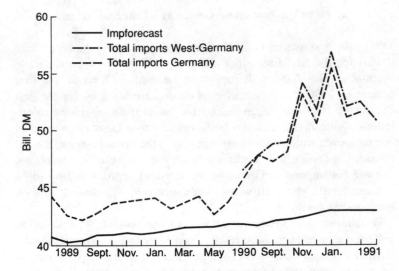

The forecast (IMPFORECAST) was based on the following regression result:

Imports = constant + 3.5* real exchange rate + 0.18* domestic demand
                        (3.2)   (9.3)

t-statistics in parenthesis, $R^2 = 0.96$, DW = 2.09, the equation included a moving average
(-0.5) and an autoaggressive (0.93) term. (t-statistics: -4.6 and 13.9 respectively).

Figure 1 shows that the actual import values start to diverge considerably from the forecast in early 1990. By the end of that year the
difference between actual and the forecast for West German imports

reaches about 10 billion deutsche mark per month. This suggests that unification has a large effect on import demand which goes well beyond the indirect effect coming from the boom in West Germany since the latter can explain only a small part of the actual increase in imports.

The direct effect of unification on import demand is estimated at somewhat more than 8 billion deutsche mark per month, on average, for the last quarter of 1990. If it continues at that rate the trade account for 1991 might in fact be in deficit.

It is also apparent from Figure 1 that a large residual would remain even if one assumes that income in the five new *Länder* is about 10% of West German income since that would increase the forecast values for imports only by about 10% i.e. from about 40 to 44 billion deutsche mark per month (the income elasticity is about 1). Actual imports are, however, almost 20% higher than one would expect given the past relationship between imports and domestic demand in West Germany.

Another interesting issue that can be elucidated with this method is to what extent the increase in German imports benefits its partners in the European Community. The increase in German interest rates has forced other EMS participants to raise domestic interest rates as well. This is felt as a burden by Germany's European partners, but one should set the increase in German imports against the interest rate effect.

The beneficial effects of unification on Germany's EC partners can be estimated by applying the same method to the demand for imports coming from outside the Community. This is done in Gros (1991) who finds that the residuals for non-EC imports are close to 4 billion deutsche mark on average for the last quarter of 1990 and early 1991. This suggests that about one half of the additional imports caused by unification come from outside the Community (and the other half from partner countries inside). This is the distribution one would have expected anyway given that about one half of German imports come from the Community. Extrapolating this trend to 1991 implies that the German intra-EC surplus should diminish by about 50 billion deutsche mark during the current year (or that other EC countries will receive a demand boost equal to almost 1% of their combined GDP).

The shift in the German important demand function has, if it turns out to be permanent, one important policy implication: it confirms our view that there is no need for an adjustment of exchange rates within the EMS (and against the dollar) to reduce the German current account surplus.

Import (and export) demand functions are certainly not the only, or even the main factors that determine the exchange rate. But our findings nevertheless suggest that the German external position can undergo large swings without requiring large exchange rate adjustments.

4. Conclusion

German unification leads to large shifts of demand and also to large factor movements within one small area that constitutes an economic and monetary union. This requires large shifts of relative prices within Germany. But these are possible (at least in one direction) since, due to the exceptional circumstances, wages can move independently in the two regions of the German EMU. The purpose of this essay is to argue that the need for a change in the relative price of goods produced in one part of Germany (the western part), relative to the price of goods in the rest of Europe, will be minor.

There is certainly no need for a large real appreciation of the deutsche mark. On the contrary, as demand by households in West Germany is reduced by higher taxes the deutsche mark should remain weak in the EMS, and inflation (in West Germany) should also remain moderate.

If the arguments used by others to justify the need for a real appreciation of the deutsche mark were correct, it would follow by analogy that, once an Economics and Monetary Union is established in the EC, any large increase in regional aid that finances large public investment in the South of Europe should lead to a strengthening of the (single European) currency. It seems unlikely that many would accept this corollary.

APPENDIX

This appendix provides the analytical model that underlies the verbal reasoning of the main text. The model used here can be found in many textbooks, see e.g. Dornbusch (1980), chapter 6. The model is based on a set of excess demand equations for non-tradables, denoted by $N(.)$. The resulting equilibrium conditions are as follows:

(1) $0 = N(s/^{w}p_{N}, {}^{w}E)$ (for West Germany)
(2) $0 = N(s/^{e}p_{N}, {}^{e}E)$ (for East Germany)

Excess demand for non-tradables depends on the relative price of tradables to non-tradables *in the region concerned* because the price of non-tradables, denoted by ${}^{w}p_{N}$ and ${}^{e}p_{N}$ respectively, can move independently in the two parts of Germany as argued in the text. Excess demand is given by the difference between demand and supply. Demand for non-tradables is an increasing function and their supply is a decreasing function of the relative price of tradables, s/p_{N}. The derivative of $N(.)$ with respect to s/p_{N} is thus positive. Demand for non-tradables is also an increasing function of overall real expenditure in the two regions, denoted by ${}^{w}E$ and ${}^{e}E$, respectively. Equilibrium in the market for non-tradables requires the excess demand in both areas to be equal to zero because they cannot be traded between the two regions of Germany.

However, the price of tradables has to be the same in the two parts of Germany. The exchange rate, s, represents the number of DM per ecu. Assuming that the ecu price of tradables is not affected by what is going on in Germany, s thus also represents the price of tradables and the ratio s/p_{N} represents the real exchange rate. It is usually assumed that the price of non-tradables is proportional to wages. This implies in the present context that the price of West German non-tradables is also given if nominal West German wages are given. This assumption is reflected in the bar in the expression ${}^{w}p_{N}$. However, as argued in the text, wages in the eastern part of Germany are flexible, at least upwards.

Using West German wages as the numeraire merely keeps the exposition as simple as possible. The results would not be affected if a system of money demand and supplies were added so that the general price level would be determined by the monetary policy of the Bundesbank. Indeed, if the Bundesbank sticks to its monetary target the average wage level in Germany would be pinned down and any increase in East Germany would have to be accompanied by a decrease in West Germany, thus creating pressures for a devaluation of the DM (which reinforces our point).

The two equations (1) and (2) determine jointly the exchange rate and the price of non-tradables in East Germany with the latter equal to the 'East German real exchange rate'. It is apparent that, given real expenditure in West Germany, equation (1) alone determines the exchange rate and that if ^wE does not change there is no reason why s should change.

The result that there is no need for an appreciation of the DM follows thus immediately from the (documented) assumption about the behaviour of West German expenditure. Moreover, as argued in the text, if West Germans spend less now because they expect taxes to go up in the future, s would even have to increase (if ^wE goes down s has to increase in equation (1)), i.e. the DM would have to be devalued. In East Germany there is the usual effect that an increase in real expenditure will lead to an increase in the price of non-tradables and thus implicitly to an appreciation of the real exchange rate of the 'East German DM'.

This extremely simple model could, of course, be generalized in a variety of ways. The most obvious one is that real expenditure is itself a function of the real exchange rate since it is given by the sum of expenditure on tradables and non-tradables:

$$(3)\ ^wE \equiv\ ^wN + (s/^wp_N)^wT$$

$$(4)\ ^eE \equiv\ ^eN + (s/^ep_N)^eT$$

where ^wN and ^eN represent the demand for non-tradables in west and east Germany respectively and ^wT and ^eT do the same for tradables. However, as shown in Dornbusch (1980) this generalization does not affect the previous results as long as the substitution effects in (1) and (2) are stronger than the income effects operating through equations (3) and (4). However, Dornbusch (1980) also shows how the model can be built up from microfoundations, and how it can be enriched by assuming tradables are no longer perfect substitutes.

References

Akerlof, G. A. et al., (1991), 'East Germany in from the Cold: The Economic Aftermath of Currency Union', draft, March.

Artus, P. (1991), 'Réunification allemande, dynamique et contraintes: un cadre d'analyse' Caisse des dépôts et consignation, Paris, January.

Basevi, G. (1990), 'Some implications of the development of Eastern Europe for the European Economic and Monetary Union', Manuscript, University of Bologna, Bologna.

Burda, M. (1990), 'Les conséquences de l'union économique et monétaire de l'Allemagne', in Fitoussi, J. P. (ed.) (1990) '*A l'Est en Europe*, Paris: Presses de la Fondation National des Sciences Politiques.

Dornbusch, R. (1980), 'Employment, the trade balance and relative prices', chapter 3 in *Open Economy Macroeconomics*, New York: Basic Books.

Fitoussi, J. P. (ed.) (1990) '*A l'Est en Europe*, Paris: Presses de la Fondation National des Sciences Politiques.

Fitoussi, J. P. and E. Phelps (1990), 'Note sur les conséquences globales de la reconstruction de l'Europe de l'Est et de l'épargne mondiale, in Fitoussi, J. P. (ed.) (1990) '*A l'Est en Europe*, Paris: Presses de la Fondation National des Sciences Politiques.

Gros, D. (1991), 'The effects of unification on the German current account', Centre for European Policy Studies, unpublished manuscript, May.

Gros, D. and A. Steinherr (1990), 'Currency union and economic reform in the GDR: a comprehensive one-step approach', in *German Unification in European Perspective*, Centre for European Policy Studies, *CEPS Working Document*, 49, Brussels.

Hoffmann, L. (1990), 'Wider die okonomische Vernunft', *Frankfurter Allgemeine Zeitung*, 10 February.

International Monetary Fund (1990) *German Unification: Economic Issues*, Occasional Paper, International Monetary Fund, Washington, DC.

MacKibbin, W. (1990), 'Some global macroeconomic implications of German unification', *Brookings Discussion Papers in International Economics*, 81, Washington, DC.

Sachverständigenrat, (1990), 'Bedenken der Sachverstandigen gegen Wahrungsunion', *Frankfurter Allgemeine Zeitung* 10 February.

Schatz, K-W., and Schmidt, (1991), 'German economic integration: real economic adjustment of the East German economy in the short and in the long run', paper prepared for the Kiel conference on *The Transformation of Socialist Economies*, 26–28 June.

Schlesinger, H. (1990), 'Mit sofortiger Währungsunion lassen sich das wirklichen Probleme nicht beheben', *Handelsblatt*, 24 January.

Siebert H. (1991), 'The integration of Germany: Real economic adjustment', *European Economic Review*, in press.

Walter, N. (1991), 'German Monetary Union—Experiences and Problems' International Economic Conference on 'Building the New Europe', Rome, 7-9 January.

Wyplosz, Ch. (1991), 'On the real exchange rate effect of German unification', *Weltwirtschaftliches Archiv*.

66   *Daniel Gros and Alfred Steinherr*

Notes

1 See Sachverständigenrat (1990), Hoffmann (1990) and Schlesinger (1990).
2 Opponents of currency union see confirmation of their analysis in the sharp reductions in production and employment in the ex-GDR. The fall in industrial production is estimated in excess of 50% (Akerlof et al., (1991)). However, this may have been unavoidable as illustrated by the 40% decline in industrial production in the US between 1945 and 1947 caused by the changing structure of demand in a peace economy (Schatz and Schmidt (1991)). And it is clear that what has happened in the ex-GDR is a drastic shift in demand away from home goods. This shift could not have been prevented by devaluation and was not prevented by an actual fall in producer prices in excess of 50% (Akerlof et al.).
3 Quite remarkably East Germans are not changing their savings behaviour dramatically, as evidenced in Table 1. The modest decline in M3 is compatible with a rather slow process of substitution into other financial and real assets not available until unification.
4 If East Germans have the same marginal rate to save and spend at margin the same share of expenditures on West German and on non-German goods as do West Germans (assumptions which seem close to reality), then the intra-German transfer has no external effect other than via non-tradable goods prices. See Dornbusch (1980), chapter 3. The massive transfer of deutsche mark 65 billion in 1990 and deutsche mark 90-100 billion in 1999 (see Walter (1991)) contributes therefore to a real depreciation of the deutsche mark.
5 This argument does not mean that in the case of Germany 'full Ricardian equivalence' applies and that therefore all future taxes are immediately taken into account by consumers. All it implies is that in the present special circumstances the German public is very well aware of the burden on the public finances that will come over the next years. This public awareness, coupled with higher interest rates should dampen expenditure in West Germany.
6 That is the West German CPI should increase less. However, the weighted average of the East and West German CPI can be expected to show a much higher inflation rate since wages in East Germany should increase at a faster rate than wages in the West.
7 These crude calculations do not take into account the import content of West German exports into the GDR, which has been estimated to be as high as 40%, implying that each mark of exports from West to East Germany reduces the current account surplus by 0.4 mark. However, preliminary calculations suggest that this effect is more or less offset by the fact that exports from the rest of the Community (and EFTA) contain imports from the FRG.

8 The demand side story takes place implicitly at given factor endowments.

9 Perfect, i.e. instantaneous, mobility of both factors would, of course, lead to instant equalization of the capital labour ratio. However, since movements of both factors involve adjustment costs the capital labour ratio will not be equalized immediately.

10 In this equation monthly import value(s) are determined by domestic nominal demand and the real exchange rate, using data from 1979/02 to 1989/12.

Exchange Rate Management When There Are Failures of Corporate Control: Dilemmas in Eastern Europe

SPECIAL MERIT AWARD

Summary

Should real exchange rates in the formerly planned economies be kept low during the transition to a market economy so as to encourage expansion by firms producing exports and goods that compete with imports? Or should they be kept fairly high so that the threat of losing business to imports forces sleepy state monopolies out of their inertia? The sobering lesson of 1990 in Eastern Europe has been that both strategies are highly dangerous: if firms are not used to responding to profit opportunities in a recognisably competitive manner, the economic consequences of any theoretically optimal exchange rate regime may be disappointing or even perverse. In Poland, an undervalued real exchange rate did not prevent the state enterprise sector from reducing its output by 25% during 1990; in Eastern Germany, an overvaluation of the Ostmark at the time of monetary union did not discourage already uncompetitive firms from awarding high real wage increases to their workers and worsening their competitiveness problems still further. The explanation of both of these developments lies in the failures of corporate control that characterise the structure of enterprises inherited from the era of central planning. And identifying the precise sources of competitive behaviour among enterprises may be essential before exchange rates can be managed effectively in any of the reforming economies.

Paul B. Seabright is Fellow and Director of Studies in Economics at Churchill College, Cambridge. He is a research fellow of the Centre for Economic Policy Research and an assistant editor of the journal *Economic Policy*. His research interests include the study of financial markets, the regulation of industry, and policy issues in developing countries. He has recently been studying economic restructuring in Poland and Germany, partly as a member of a team, advising the Polish government on a project funded by the UK Knowhow Fund.

5
Exchange Rate Management When There Are Failures of Corporate Control: Dilemmas in Eastern Europe

PAUL B. SEABRIGHT

Introduction

Should real exchange rates in the formerly planned economies be kept low during the transition to a market economy so as to encourage expansion by firms producing exports and goods that compete with imports? Or should they be kept fairly high so that the threat of losing business to imports forces sleepy state monopolies out of their complacent sloth? The sobering lesson of 1990 in Eastern Europe has been that both strategies are highly dangerous: if firms are not used to responding to profit opportunities in a recognisably competitive manner, the economic consequences of any theoretically optimal exchange rate regime may be disappointing or even perverse. In Poland, an undervalued real exchange rate did not prevent the state enterprise sector from reducing its output by 25 during 1990; in Eastern Germany, an overvaluation of the Ostmark at the time of monetary union did not discourage already uncompetitive firms from awarding high real wage increases to their workers and worsening their competitiveness problems still further. The explanation of both of these developments lies in the failures of corporate control that characterise the structure of enterprises inherited from the era of central planning. And identifying the precise sources of uncompetitive behaviour among enterprises may be essential before exchange rates can be managed effectively in any of the reforming economies.

An Undervalued Exchange Rate: the Polish Case

In January 1990, as part of the 'Big Bang', Poland devalued the zloty to a rate of 9,500 to the US dollar. Since this was roughly equivalent to the weakest previous unofficial rate of the currency (and was weaker than the December 1989 unofficial rate of 7,500) it seems likely that it represented a significant undervaluation of the zloty—perhaps by as much as 50% of purchasing power parity—and an undervaluation that persisted for most of 1990. The motivation for this low real exchange rate policy was not straightforward: partly it was a desire to ensure that the nominal rate could be held for long enough to lend credibility to the anti-inflationary programme as a whole; partly it was the result of genuine uncertainty as to where an equilibrium exchange might lie. But in part at least it reflected an appreciation by policymakers that the lessons of adjustment policies elsewhere in the world were largely favourable to the option of maintaining real exchange rates at levels conducive to the competitiveness of domestic producers of tradable goods and services. The export-led growth of the newly-industrialising countries of East Asia had been characterised by fairly low real exchange rates. More negatively, the experiences of some Latin American economies with simultaneous macroeconomic stabilisation and microeconomic liberalisation (especially of financial markets) pointed to the serious dangers posed by overvalued real exchange rates.[1] These countries had seen their tradable goods sectors crushed between the pincers of high domestic inflation and an unwillingness to devalue nominal exchange rates for fear of compromising anti-inflationary credibility. One consequence of this experience had been a broad consensus among academics and policymakers on the so-called 'tariffs first' approach to external liberalisation. The tariffs first approach consists of a recommendation that capital account convertibility be delayed until the export sector has expanded under the impact of trade liberalisation, for fear that an inflow of capital seeking profitable investment opportunities will make real exchange rate appreciation unavoidable. This approach was influential in the design of Poland's liberalisation policies, for convertibility of the zloty was established only for commercial and not for portfolio transactions (though individual residents may hold dollar-denominated deposit accounts). It is clear that, given annual zloty interest rates of 70% for most of 1990 and dollar rates of less than 10%, full convertibility in the presence of a commitment not to devalue the nominal exchange rate would have led to large-scale capital inflows and a rapid correction of the initial undervaluation. Resistance to full convertibility was therefore based very much on the perceived need for competitiveness in tradable goods production.

In theory this should have led to an expansion of output in the tradable sectors of the economy. And indeed recorded industrial output in the private sector rose by an estimated 8.5% in 1990, much of this on the back of a rise of a third in exports to the convertible currency economies; the true (unrecorded) rise in output was almost certainly substantially higher. But the industrial output of the state enterprise sector fell by 25% in 1990. Why?

The explanation cannot lie wholly or even mainly in a difference in the kinds of output produced by the state and the private sectors, since the fall in state sector output was greatest in precisely those industries—clothing and household durable goods—that competed most directly with private producers. By far the most likely explanation is the difference in the incentive structures within private sector and state sector firms. Private sector firms in Poland are more directed towards the pursuit of profitable activities, and tend to face a more competitive environment: for them the increase in relative profitability of tradable goods production resulting from the low real exchange rate was an attractive and effective incentive. Many state sector enterprises, by contrast, operate in markets whose degree of concentration is extraordinarily high by the standards of the industrialized market economies.[2] Firms enjoy substantial monopoly power, which gave them the ability to raise prices to well above the competitive level once price-setting was liberalised at the start of 1990. Indeed, as simple microeconomic theory would predict, they raised their prices to a level at which demand fell (by some 30% in little over a month for the output of the state sector). This development was exacerbated by the grossly uncompetitive nature of the banking sector, which meant that although loan rates rose to 48% per month in January 1990, deposit rates reached only 22% on a monthly basis, leaving an extraordinary spread of 26 percentage (not basis!) points per month. This spread, combined with high interest rates on loans and a mismatch between assets and liabilities meant that enterprises were caught in a savage liquidity squeeze—which they could use their monopoly power to pass on to consumers. Rough calculations suggest that in January 1990 alone enterprises faced additional net interest outflows of 9.4 trillion zlotys, or more than 15% of monthly GDP.[3] Much of the burden of these outflows must have fallen ultimately on consumers, for although enterprise profitability fell at the beginning of 1990, this was only from the unusually high levels of late 1989, and during 1990 profitability compared favourably with its levels in the first three quarters of 1989.

Indeed, the fact that this was so during a period when output was on average 25% below its 1989 level suggests that mark-ups on costs *per unit* must have risen by 25-30% after liberalization, which is very much what the monopoly power of firms would lead one to expect.[4]

Even if state enterprises were able to reap substantial monopoly profits from the new freedom conferred on them by price liberalisation, the increased relative profitability of tradable goods production might have been expected to lead them to increase rather than reduce output in pursuit of export opportunities. In fact, unlike private firms they remained largely unmoved by these opportunities. The fact that reasonably comfortable profits were assured in domestic markets for many state firms meant that they could postpone restructuring decisions and the risky attempt to conquer new markets abroad. This was not simply a psychological peculiarity of state enterprises, but an entirely natural result of their being still managed by workers' councils and having limited managerial discretion or incentives.

Poland's experience in 1990 strongly suggests, therefore, that the response of firms to a particular real exchange rate depends ultimately on whether their most effective incentive to restructure their operations is the prospect of profits in new activities, or the fear of liquidation if they remain in their old ones. The answer to this will depend in turn on how well the internal structure of firms is oriented toward the pursuit of profitable activities. At present this seems to be so to a considerable extent in private sector firms, but hardly at all in the enterprises owned by the state. Exchange rate policies will therefore tend to have differential effects on the private and state enterprise sectors. A low exchange rate, other things equal, might be expected to favour the growth of the private sector at the cost of diminishing the credibility of the threat faced by the state sector and therefore enabling it to delay restructuring. A comparatively firm exchange rate will be less favourable to the private sector, but will correspondingly place greater pressure on state enterprises to adapt in spite of their enjoyment of substantial domestic market power.

The idea that the restructuring of the Polish economy can take place purely by expansion of the existing price sector (the 'withering away of the state sector', to echo the old Marxist phrase) is hardly credible. Even at the end of the 1990 the private sector accounted for less than 15% of industrial output.[5] But waiting until all state enterprises have been privatised is likely to delay the restructuring process longer than is desirable or politically tolerable. This suggests a rather pointed lesson for the Polish economy. The sooner state enterprises can be internally restructured (while still publicly owned), so that their managements have a genuine incentive to seek out new profitable opportunities rather than continuing to rest on the laurels of their market power, the sooner macroeconomic management can afford to be based on a policy of an attractively low real exchange rate. Conversely, the longer managers of state enterprises can remain in a corporate environment where they benefit from inertia, the more a relatively uncompetitive real exchange rate policy will be required to enforce the credible threat of liquidation unless they adapt.

An observer looking just at Poland's experience might therefore conclude that, since major restructuring of the state enterprise sector will take some time to achieve, the failure of firms in this sector to respond adequately to indicators of relative profitability makes it necessary to maintain a reasonably high real exchange rate. On this view, lessons from East Asia and Latin America are of limited applicability: those economies, for all their distortions, had a greater degree of domestic competition and a more substantial and profit oriented private sector than any of the former command economies. Correspondingly, the 'tariffs-first' policy may have been a mistake when applied to Poland: some capital inflow might have corrected the initial undervaluation of 1990, and faced domestic firms with a credible incentive to cut costs and restructure their activities. Such an observer might take the United Kingdom in the early 1980s as a more appropriate example of the effects of overvaluation than either Chile or Argentina: although having a major depressant effect on industrial output, the UK's overvaluation played an important role, according to sympathetic critics, in bringing about the shake-out of inefficient activities encouraged by years of accommodating exchange rate management. This would not (even to those sympathetic critics) imply that a permanently overvalued exchange rate were desirable even if it were possible. But it could imply that it was a necessary temporary feature of a 'shock therapy' designed to root out embedded inefficiency in industrial organisation.

Unfortunately, experience elsewhere in Eastern Europe[6] suggests that those very failures of corporate control that have led to perverse responses to a low real exchange rate might equally hinder the reaction of firms to a high rate. The fate of Eastern Germany after monetary union is a case in point.

An Overvalued-Exchange Rate: the East German Case

At the beginning of July 1990, the Federal Republic of Germany and
the German Democratic Republic formed a monetary union, as a
preliminary step towards full political union later that year. Ostmarks
(the currency of the GDR) were converted into Deutschmarks at a rate
of one for one, for the purposes of determining relative wage rates and
the prices of goods and services (conversions of capital sums were
made according to a more complex formula). It seemed likely at the
time that this represented a significant overvaluation of the Ostmark,
given the relative productivity of the workforce in the two countries,
working as they were with stocks of capital of vastly different quality.
Few observers, however, anticipated the dramatic collapse of the
output of East German firms, which fell by 35% in the month
following monetary union, and by December of 1990 had reached
45.5% of its 1989 level. Fewer still can have anticipated the response
of East German firms to these developments. Far from seeking to cut
costs and restrain wage levels, as might be expected in a reasonably
competitive economy responding to an unexpected overvaluation of its
currency, East German firms continued to pay substantial wage
increases. That is, they paid increases above the already dramatically
competitive levels resulting from monetary union. The consequence
was an intensification of what was already one of the deepest
recessions in history, and the effective insolvency of most of the
industry of the former GDR.[7]

If nothing else, the East German experience shows that the problem
for exchange rate policy is not simply that of establishing the complete
credibility of a chosen nominal rate. Indeed, the lesson of that
experience could be summarised, echoing Edith Cavell, as 'credibility
is not enough'. What could have been more credible than the policy of
monetary union? Nobody in either East or West Germany ever thought
that monetary union might be reversed or the conversion rates retro-
spectively changed. And yet firms have continued to pay out rising real
wages even though the parity chosen at monetary union was one at
which most enterprises were already seriously uncompetitive. What
appears to have happened is that the incentives of workers have been to
press for higher wage rises (partly because of the way the West
German unemployment benefit system links benefit levels to final
wages), and managers have had little incentive to resist them. While

some of these features (such as the generous benefit system) may not be directly applicable to other countries in Eastern Europe, they underline the general point that even a credible liquidation threat may not have the desired effect upon firm behaviour unless those who work in an enterprise feel they have something genuinely to gain from keeping the enterprise going.

If managers and workers in a firm believe that the probability of their facing bankruptcy is low, they will quite reasonably devote most of their energies to making the best of their involvement in the enterprise as a going concern. In most circumstances (and given reliable auditing procedures) that will mean acting to ensure the profitable and efficient management of the firm's assets. But if managers and workers become convinced that bankruptcy is either inevitable or at least highly likely, they will then—and no less reasonably—devote most of their attention to ensuring that the firm goes bankrupt in the manner most favourable to themselves. That may mean paying high wages and salaries in the meantime. It may mean disposing of assets to their own benefit. It is unlikely to mean managing assets in the most profitable manner, since the profits from doing so will accrue to precisely those stakeholders in the firm (owners of equity and debt) who are not represented in the firm's day-to-day management decisions.

The explanation for the behaviour of German enterprises is undoubtedly a complex one (West German unions such as IG Metall were partly responsible for pressing high wage claims on disorganised and demoralised East German management). But the divorce between the interests of enterprises and the interests of their managers was a striking contributor to the serious developments in the East. If Poland's experience demonstrates that failures of corporate control can frustrate the impact of a low real exchange rate, that of Eastern Germany shows that they can result in an entirely perverse reaction to an overvalued rate. What can be done about such failures? And what conclusions can be drawn for exchange rate policy?

Conclusions

It is easier to see what ought to be done about the failures of corporate control in the Polish than in the East German case. Polish state enterprises have been failing to respond to opportunities for profitable production of tradable goods and services, because they have been failing to respond to profitable opportunities of any kind. What is needed is a structure of incentives within Polish enterprises that rewards successful initiative and makes managerial appointments conditional on performance. Competition policy will also need to ensure that managers can pursue profitable performance by efficiently managing corporate assets rather than by exploiting market power. Such a structure of incentives cannot wait for privatization to happen but must be implemented as soon as possible. Even so, it will take time, and in the meanwhile state enterprises tempted to enjoy the quiet life need to realise that their life may not remain quiet for very much longer. A reasonably firm exchange rate is more or less inescapable in these circumstances: what went wrong in Eastern Germany was not that the policy of overvaluation was misguided in principle but that it was drastically excessive in practice. Continuing inflation in Poland has, however, meant that, in spite of a small devaluation in May 1991, enterprise profitability has slumped, many potentially efficient firms face a liquidity crisis, and (as of August 1991) non-performing loans from commercial banks have risen to nearly 10% of outstanding credit. This suggests, therefore, that the present real exchange rate may now have exceeded the limits of tolerable overvaluation and that Poland in 1991 risks looking much more like East Germany in 1990 than like Poland in 1990.

   No feasible system of corporate control can realistically hope to avoid perverse enterprise behaviour in the face of a collapse as dramatic as that of the East German economy in 1990. If 80% of managers believe the firms will be bankrupt, they will not act to manage the existing assets as efficiently as possible: this would be true in Japan or in the United States, no less than in Germany. There are some partial lessons from the events of 1990: Germany could have done more to ensure that existing workers and managers had a stake in their enterprises (perhaps by a clear promise of equity participation in successfully privatised firms); the payment of unemployment benefit could have been delinked from final salaries. But the main lesson is that competition from imports, though strong enough to be credible, must not be so strong as to be overwhelming. The real exchange rate must not be allowed to climb more than a little above a realistically competitive level. And the sooner the structure of corporate control can be reformed to encourage firms to respond to new profit opportunities, the sooner exchange rate management can afford to favour the development of foreign trade.

Much intellectual energy is now being devoted to devising mechanisms for implementing private ownership of the assets of Eastern Europe's state enterprises. There is justifiable concern that the benefits from ownership of these assets should be distributed fairly, and without prejudice to their efficient management. Arguments are developing about the appropriate mechanisms and corporate control to ensure that efficient management, and in particular about the relative merits of stock markets on the Anglo-American pattern, and universal banks on the German pattern. These arguments, important as they are, are hampered by the lack of firm evidence that the disappointing economic performance of the US and the UK in the post war era, in comparison with that of the more bank-dominated economies of Germany and Japan, has anything to do with these countries' financial systems, as opposed to differences in their labour force and their business culture. It is hard to know, therefore, how much the design of systems of corporate control matters for long-term growth, and how much failures of corporate control can be blamed for a poor growth performance. By contrast, there is no doubt whatever that responses to major macroeconomic shocks, such as those now buffeting Eastern Europe, depend very critically on the effectiveness with which managers of enterprises are monitored and controlled; it is in moments of stress and turmoil that inventive, adaptable management really becomes important. To put it another way, remedying failures of corporate control in Eastern Europe is not just a medium-term problem. The nature of the reforming economies' response to exchange rate policies today depends critically on the nature of their enterprise management, and on the degree to which failures in monitoring that management can be easily and speedily rectified.

Notes and References

1 Sebastian Edwards has discussed the Latin American precedent in 'Stabilization and Liberalization Policies in Central and Eastern Europe: Lessons from Latin America', University of California, Los Angeles, mimeo.
2 This is a well documented phenomenon (e.g. by Mark Schaffer in 'State-owned Enterprises in Poland', *The European Economy*, March 1990); David

78 *Paul B. Seabright*

Newbery makes similar observations about Hungary and Yugoslavia in 'Competition Policy in Eastern Europe', University of Cambridge, Department of Applied Economics discussion paper, April 1991.

3 I am grateful to Christopher Allsopp of New College, Oxford, and Harry Bingham of the European Bank for Reconstruction and Development for these calculations, which are based on statistics from GUS, Warsaw.

4 It should be stressed that the nature of the accounting conventions means that enterprise profits are a very unreliable guide to profits in the economic sense. Nevertheless, changes in profitability might be expected to capture in a useful way the extent to which costs and prices are moving in similar or different directions. Enterprises in 1990 were not only paying much higher interest charges than in 1989 but had also seen the removal of most state subsidies. Non-labour costs had therefore risen dramatically, and the fact that markups per unit had also risen indicates strongly that firms were simultaneously benefiting from new opportunities to exploit market power. A recent paper by Mark Schaffer, however, argues that profitability was rising sharply during the 2nd half of 1989, and that the fall in output in January 1990 cannot be explained solely by the exploitation of market power, but was partly due to the demand shock arising from the sharp fall in real wages ('A Note On the Polish State-Owned Enterprise Sector in 1990', London School of Economics, mimeo).

5 This is based on estimates made by the Central Statistical Office in Warsaw; they may be on the low side, but not so much as to invalidate the general argument.

6 And even in the UK, according to unsympathetic critics of the Thatcher overvaluation.

7 George Akerlof et al. have estimated that only 8% of East German industry can cover even its variable costs at existing real wages and at world prices for inputs and outputs ('East Germany in from the Cold: the Economic Aftermath of Currency Union', paper presented at the Brookings Panel on Economic Activity, April 1990).

Integrating Eastern Europe into a Wider Europe

SPECIAL MERIT AWARD

Summary

The emerging democracies of Eastern Europe present a challenge to Western Europe. The nature of that challenge is to aid transformation from totalitarian communism to democratic pluralism and a market economy.

Western Europe has a close interest in a successful transition for reasons of political stability on its Eastern border and economic opportunity in new markets.

For purposes of the paper, Western European policy is taken to be EC policy. The Community's chosen instrument for economic relations with Eastern Europe is association agreements known as the Europe Agreements. These offer industrial free trade and the 'approximation of laws', leading to freedom of movement of goods, services, capital and labour, to aid, and to economic, political and cultural cooperation. They are open to all East Europeans but are initially being negotiated with Czechoslovakia, Hungary and Poland.

The provisions of the Europe Agreements are well-designed to deal with the issues facing Eastern Europe, but they are flawed in detail. Industrial free trade excludes textiles and steel and the CAP applies to agriculture. Anti-dumping, selective safeguards and rules of origin all threaten trade opportunities and direct investment. Approximation of laws is too slow and offers regulation without representation.

To rectify this the Community should liberalise textiles, steel, agriculture; clarify and preferably drop anti-dumping, safeguards and onerous rules of origin in the presence of effective competition policy in Eastern Europe; and speed up approximation of laws. These are all difficult in the light of domestic pressure groups. The alternative is to treat Association as a staging post to membership rather than, as now, an alternative to it. The real challenge for the Community then is to prepare itself to become a truly European construction.

Jim Rollo gained his B.Sc. in Economics and Agricultural Economics from Glasgow University and his M.Sc. in Economics from the London School of Economics. He spent more than 20 years as a British Government economist, working first in the Ministry of Agriculture, subsequently in the Overseas Development Administration and finally in the Foreign and Commonwealth Office. He joined the Royal Institute of International Affairs as Head of the International Economics Programme in November 1989. His main research interests are trade policy, the European Community and the formerly socialist economies of Central and Eastern Europe. Since joining Chatham House, he has contributed to and edited a Chatham House paper 'The New Eastern Europe: Western Responses', published a discussion paper on agriculture in the GATT and a paper on Polish economic reform.

6

Integrating Eastern Europe into a Wider Europe

JAMES M. C. ROLLO

The emerging democracies of Eastern Europe[1] present a challenge to Western Europe. The nature of the challenge is simply stated. It is to aid Eastern Europe to move from totalitarian communism to democratic pluralism and a market economy. This would entail with it an integration of Eastern Europe into what has become the post-war Western European norm. The challenge is essentially a practical one. There is no experience of making the change from a completely totalitarian system with all markets driven underground and criminalised to one where the final test of an economic transaction is a market test.

The Reform Process in Eastern Europe

There is a burgeoning literature on the reform process, mainly on the economic aspects.[2] The generally acknowledged problems fall into short and long term. The short term problem differs among the six countries of Central (Czechoslovakia, Hungary and Poland) and South East Europe (Bulgaria, Romania and Yugoslavia). Overall however they all face the need for macro-economic stabilisation to a greater or lesser extent in order to reduce inflation and to bring about a sustainable external position.

The long term economic reforms are common to all of the countries and revolve around the issue of how to reintroduce the market into economies where it has been absent in any except the most distorted form for two generations. At the institutional level this requires the introduction of competition into the economy. This in turn demands the freeing of prices; the ending of extensive subsidy to enterprises and in trade; the opening of borders to imports and freedom to export; a currency which is convertible at least in respect to current account transactions; and, as quickly as practicable, the privatisation of state firms and assets.

The effectiveness of this long term reform will depend on the creation of a legal system which guarantees the right to property and supports that by civil laws and courts which allow commercial contracts to be maintained and disputes settled. It also requires a panoply of regulations which cover competition, financial institutions, goods, services and labour markets, all necessary for the smooth functioning of competitive processes. Also necessary in the short and long term are social safety nets to protect those worst affected by the transition and significant shifts in income distribution over the longer term.

Political pluralism is the key to the economic reform so far. The shift from Communist systems resulted from pressure from the streets. If the inevitably long and risky process of economic reform is to be successful, political institutions which have the confidence of the people and transmit their views to policy makers accurately are required for the future. Democratic pluralism seems the most effective means of ensuring consent. There is no guarantee, however, that democracy will deliver effective economic policy.

The Interest of Western Europe in Economic Reform in Eastern Europe

The Western European interest in the reforms in the countries of Central and South East Europe is a mixture of altruism and self-interest. The altruism is based on the wish to respond to the ultimate flattery in which former enemies acknowledge the superiority of democracy and the market economy after 45 years of Communism.

The hard-headed motives are economic and political. The economic motive is that these countries represent a resource and a market; a resource in the sense that they have a well educated work force employed in a vastly inefficient way; a market, as another 110 million people with an expected purchasing power per head of the same order as Greece has now, within 10 or 15 years if reforms go well, add to European consumption. In the meantime they represent a market for capital goods.

The political reasons are twofold. The first is linked to the success of the economic reforms. If they fail there is likely to be a significant movement of labour from Central and South East Europe to the West. Whatever the benefits of this in economic terms (lower real wages, higher output, better competitiveness) the political problems of a vast illegal immigration will be extremely difficult to manage. Western Europe thus has a direct interest in helping reforms to succeed.

Secondly, on the political side, there is the issue of the impact of instability in the East. Nationalist pressures and economic collapse could lead to unrest and even civil strife in these countries. It might also lead to border disputes escalating. This sort of instability would be unsettling for the EC states on their borders, not least because of the refugee/emigration issue raised by civil unrest.

Which Western Europe?

The effective definition of Western Europe used here is the European Community. This is not a question of size alone. The countries of EFTA (Austria, Finland, Iceland, Norway, Sweden, Switzerland (and Liechtenstein)) are in negotiation with the EC to become part of an entity called the European Economic Area. This is essentially an extension of the four freedoms (goods, services, labour and capital) of the single market to EFTA. The EEA was initiated by the EC as an alternative to enlargement. It has become, in the course of a difficult negotiation, to be seen by the EFTAns at least as a stepping stone to membership. All except Iceland have made or are contemplating applications to join the EC. Thus more and more, either through the EEA or membership, the EC will for economic purposes be Western Europe.[3]

The Community's Response So Far: Aid and Trade

The Community has moved on two fronts already. The first is aid. Immediately following the Paris Summit of 1989 the EC Commission was given the responsibility for coordinating emergency aid—mainly food and medicines—from the OECD countries to Poland and Hungary. This programme expanded rapidly in the second half of 1989. By the end of the year the Commission had put together a programme for 1990 of 500m Ecu worth of aid for Poland and Hungary called the PHARE programme (Poland-Hungary Aid for Reconstructing the Economy). In addition it had the task of co-ordinating information on aid from the so-called G24 (the individual members of the OECD).[4] As 1990 progressed Czechoslovakia, Romania and Bulgaria were added to the list of eligible countries. Yugoslavia already had a trade and co-operation agreement dating from 1980 with the EC which included a financial protocol using EIB loans of up to 550m Ecu. Commitments under the PHARE programme rose to 850m Ecu for 1991 and 1000m Ecu for 1992 to meet more recipients and developing needs.

On trade, the Community had negotiated trade and co-operation agreements with Hungary in 1988 and with Poland at the end of 1989. These allowed for the abolition of long standing quotas against manufactured, food and agricultural goods and the granting of General System of Preference (GSP) status on a wide range of manufactured goods. Czechoslovakia and Bulgaria signed such agreements in November 1990 while the agreement with Romania (to replace the trade agreement of 1980) was signed in October 1990 but suspended until more progress on democracy was seen. These were significant concessions to the countries in receipt of them. The Community however felt that by themselves they were not enough. Thus even as agreement with Poland was being signed the Commission, largely at the instigation of the British Government, began to turn its mind to full association agreements as the most likely tool for future relations with the reforming countries.[5]

The Europe Agreements: From Aid and Trade to Economic Integration

The EC proposals for association agreements with Central and South East Europe (known as the Europe Agreements) are set out in communications from the Commission to the Foreign Affairs Council in April and August 1990 and following the agreement of a negotiating mandate in December 1990 in a non-paper issued January 1991.[6] Some alterations to the mandate were agreed at the EC General Affairs Council in May 1991. The proposals cover six main areas:

- Industrial Free Trade
- Approximation of laws leading to eventual freedom of movement of goods, services, capital and labour
- Aid
- Economic cooperation

- Political cooperation
- Cultural cooperation.

These agreements, although available in principle to all of the countries of Central and South East Europe, are conditional on evidence of progress towards economic reform and democracy. In practice, the Council of Ministers agreed with the Commission that only Poland, Hungary and Czechoslovakia have progressed sufficiently to meet these criteria. Accordingly the Commission was authorised by the December 1990 Foreign Affairs Council to open negotiations with these three countries. Yugoslavia, Bulgaria and Romania would have to wait but would be eligible if reforms progressed sufficiently.

An Assessment of the Economic Provisions—Integration or Poor Relations

In principle the EC proposals seem well suited to the needs of the Central and, eventually, South East Europeans. They offer trade access, which is by far the most important benefit[7] as only with that will the reforming countries begin to generate foreign exchange, and more importantly for the long term, inward investment. The approximation of laws, particularly of competition laws and the eventual extension of the freedom of movement of services, labour and capital, all make sense for countries trying to build a market economy from scratch. The EC's laws are the obvious ones to copy since they automatically help in the penetration of the Community which is these countries' largest and closest market. Economic cooperation gives direct Community input and resources to the process of approximation. The aid relationship will contribute to the building of modern infrastructure and to the construction of a private and public sector. It is also backed up by the stick of conditionality which may provide an important anchor for economic reform and political pluralism.

There are however, severe problems in the detail of the Community's initial position which significantly reduce the value of the Agreements to the Central Europeans.

On industrial free trade there are three distinct problems. The first relates to the effectively excluded areas of agriculture, textiles, steel and coal. These are all areas of immediate interest to the Central Europeans and where it is likely that exports could be increased most quickly. The main blockages relate to existing trade barriers—the CAP, the MFA and Steel Voluntary Export Restraints. All of these are under negotiations in other forums: CAP and MFA in the GATT and the Steel VRA's in the context of the EC agreement with the US to run down such quantitative restrictions. Nonetheless rapid and special action for the Central Europeans is necessary if the collapse in the export trade is not to become calamitous.

The second area of difficulty is on anti-dumping, safeguards and rules of origin. The first question about anti-dumping is why it is there at all if there is to be approximation of competition laws. The only economic justification for anti-dumping is that domestic competition laws cannot be made to apply to foreigners and there is a danger of predatory pricing. If domestic competition laws are applicable to foreigners—as is proposed in the Europe Agreements—then anti-dumping is redundant. Nor is it clear what regulations on anti-dumping will apply. If the EC use the rules currently in force against these countries which treat them as non-market economies then there is a serious potential problem in relation to exchange rates. In non-market economies domestic prices and costs may be heavily distorted. Hence proving that export prices are below domestic prices, or below costs, may be difficult. In those circumstances a proxy price from a producer in a market economy is used as the criterion of an economic price. To be comparable these prices have to be in the same currency and therein lies the problem. In recent years all of the countries concerned have made large devaluations. They are likely to need to maintain under-valued exchange rates to increase exports. Thus it is possible that using this rule could lead to a finding of dumping following a devaluation even though domestic costs and export prices would not justify such a finding.

Equally dangerous, because it is opaque, is the safeguards clause. The criterion set for safeguards action is severe disturbance to the economy of a contracting party. Since the Community as a whole is the contracting party it is difficult to see how trade from any of the Central Europeans could be capable of disrupting the Community economy as a whole. The implication is that if the safeguards clause is to be meaningful it must be effective at a much lower level of economic activity. This implies industrial and perhaps country level safeguards which could be extremely damaging to trade. On that basis any industry in any country of the EC could demand safeguards if an associate country becomes competitive in almost any product.

Nor are the dangers from selective trade policy all in the future. Uncertainty about trade access will discourage potential foreign investors with immediate effect.

Rules of origin also provide a potential problem. In the early stages of transition outward processing, in which semi-finished goods are completed for export, is likely to be an important source of inward investment, technology transfer and training. A rule of origin which demanded 60% local content, as in the EFTA agreement, could stop such valuable opportunities in their tracks. This would be very damaging, both immediately and in the longer term, since such outward processing relationships are often the first stage in a longer term relationship.

The final issue on access is timing. The Commission non-paper speaks of two phases of five years. It is not clear whether these two phases apply to the proposed asymmetrical liberalisation or to something else. If the first phase is indeed the period for the Community to liberalise, then this is far too long. The Central Europeans need immediate access not access in five years' time. The EC may hope that over 5 years the questions of steel, textiles and even agriculture may begin to solve themselves. But that does not absolve the Community from dealing with the pressing problems of the Central Europeans even if at the cost of domestic interest groups.

Approximation of Laws

The question of timing also arises on the proposals for approximation of laws. More importantly, these proposals, leading as they do to integration into the Common Market, raise the nature of the relationship between the EC and the states of Central and South East Europe.

The concept of two phases is in the Commission's non-paper, as in the industrial free trade chapter, but there is no reference to even the length of the phases let alone their content or their relation to the phasing of industrial free trade.

Taking the last point first, competition policy appears in both chapters. As noted above the approximation of competition laws has a bearing on anti-dumping (and indeed safeguards). It is probable that the Commission consider that legal approximation should follow industrial free trade.[8] That proposition must be questioned. The countries of Central and South East Europe do not have a set of laws covering economic regulation in place. They are writing them now from scratch. The obvious approach is to take EC laws *en bloc*, not to invent one set now and approximate to the Community later. If they do approximate now then the question is not just of when they integrate into the Common Market but how quickly they move to free industrial trade. Certainly a rapid approximation of laws makes a 10 year timetable for industrial free trade look far too long.

The approximation of laws also brings the implied relationship between the EC and the associated states closer to the surface. The process that the Community has in mind implies considerable inequality. The main examples of this are competition policy and labour market integration. But it also arises in the lack of access that the associate states will have to EC institutions.

The examples first: the associates are to adopt the EC competition rules but possibly be allowed some derogation on state aids while still being subject to antidumping regulation. The inclusion of a derogation implies some form of EC oversight of competition policy in the associate states. The maintenance of anti-dumping provisions implies that the East Europeans cannot be trusted to implement competition policy.

The labour market integration proposals are nothing of the kind. They are largely provisions to keep Central European workers out of the EC. Yet in return for this the associates have to accept EC labour laws which might be inappropriate for their level of development and their need to become competitive.

Overall therefore, the associates have to accept the acquis—which is no more than happens to a new entrant. But as with the EFTAns they have no input into the process of how that acquis is interpreted or developed. It is in effect regulation without representation.

Aid

Two questions on aid: first is it enough? and second is it given in a way which will ensure proper use of it? The answer to the first question is almost certainly that it is not enough in a gap-filling context. Commitments are set to rise to 1000m Ecu a year by 1992 for the 6 countries and disbursements will lag that by some time. Polish debt service (interest and capital repayments) alone—even after 50% forgiveness—

is likely to exceed $10bn a year for the next 5 years. Hungarian debt service is of the same order and Bulgarian is around $4bn.[9] Total capital needs could be in excess of $1000 billion over the next 10 years.[10] However that may be too simple a comparison. Aid concerns not just cash but also effectiveness. Relatively small sums of aid may increase returns to existing management and capital by multiples. The important aspect of the aid is not just its volume but that it should be well spent.

Equally important is that the aid should be planned in conjunction with the recipients. On that front the proposals are less good. Previous association agreements have had financial protocols which have proposed a financial envelope for a set period—usually five years— and a timetable for renewal. That gives the associated states a status in the negotiation. The Commission proposals however build on the PHARE programme which is part of the annual EC budget process— albeit in a multi-annual framework. Such a process gives the associated states no direct rule. It looks rather like a take it or leave it relationship.

Conclusions

At various points in this assessment of the economic provisions of the Europe Agreements the Community has been accused of promising more than it is willing to deliver. On access the unwillingness to confront domestic lobbies on agriculture, steel, textiles and coal; the safeguards and anti-dumping clauses; the dangers of rules of origin and; the remarkably long timetable all add up to a poor offer—even after the changes to the mandate in May 1991. On approximation of laws and integration into the single market, the timetable and the lack of any institutional role for the associated states suggests a one way relationship which promises more than it can deliver. Similarly the aid relationship is even more one-sided than such relationships normally are.

In the circumstances of Central and South East Europe such half-heartedness by the EC is disappointing enough. In the context of the Community's rhetoric about the historic nature of the changes and the EC's commitment to sustaining them it is doubly disappointing. The only thing that is certain about change in Central and South East Europe is that mistakes will be made, that progress may be fitful and that external commitment must therefore be long-term and full.

What can the Community do? The first and most obvious things would be to negotiate immediate increases in steel and textile quotas, aiming to phase them out in two or three years. The second thing would be to include the needs of Central and South East Europe as essential elements in the reform of the CAP and in the meantime open up significant duty and levy free quotas on products of importance to these countries—livestock products, fruit and vegetables, wine. The third thing would be adjure anti-dumping and safeguard provisions, subject to competition policy being in place, at the very least increasing the transparency of these clauses so that their use is predictable. The fourth would be to ensure that rules of origin do not block investment. The fifth would be to clarify the timetable for industrial free trade and open borders immediately on non-sensitive industrial goods. Sixth, the Community should clarify the timetable for approximation of laws and give the associated states some institutional locus in the interpretation and adaptation of EC regulation. Finally, on aid, a shift to a more traditional financial protocol would signal a longer term commitment and a more equal partnership.

Changes of this nature would signify commitment, a willingness to sacrifice and a wish for a more equal partnership, all of which would help anchor political stability, democracy and the market economy. It would also make conditionality more credible. If the carrots are not very alluring the Eastern Europeans are not going to wait to be beaten by the stick of conditionality.

The list above is long and difficult for the Community—its value is inversely related to the difficulty. If these changes are impossible then there is one thing the Community could do which would at least demonstrate long term commitment. That is to acknowledge that these agreements are not ends in themselves but rather a necessary step to full membership. Such an acknowledgement would not only recognise a reality, at least in the aspirations of the Eastern Europeans, but also provide a further buttressing of the conditionality in the agreements. Making the opening of enlargement negotiations conditional on having met all the requirements of the Europe Agreements on democracy, markets, trade and approximation of laws and putting a firm timetable on achieving various staging posts, would be an important reinforcement of forces for democracy and the market. It would also put considerable pressure on the EC to adapt itself in such a way that it can contemplate a further enlargement. This is the main challenge of change in Eastern Europe for the Community: not just how it can aid the historic changes going on there but rather how far it can prepare itself to become a community of 25 or more and hence a truly European construction.

References

CEPR—*Monitoring European Integration: The Impact of Eastern Europe*, 1990.

Collins, Susan and Dani Rodrik—*Eastern Europe and the Soviet Union in the World Economy*, IIE paper no. 32, Washington 1991.

European Economy No. 43—Economic Transformation in Hungary & Poland, March 1990.

European Economy No. 45—Stabilisation, Liberalisation and Devolution, December 1990.

European Economy, Special Edition No. 2 1991—The Path of Reform in Eastern Europe.

Granville, B. G. and J. M. C. Rollo—The Exchange Rate, Trade Policy & Systemic Change in Poland; Tokyo Club Papers No. 4 December 1990.

House of Lords—Select Committee on the European Community (HL Paper, March 1991) European Agreements with Poland & Hungary and the Czech and Slovak Federal Republic.

Kemme, David M.—Economic Transition in Eastern Europe and the Soviet Union: Issues and Strategy; Institute for East-West Security Studies Occasional Paper No. 20 May 1991.

Pinder, John—*The European Community and Eastern Europe*, Pinter Publishers for the Royal Institute for International Affairs (RIIA), (July 1991).

Rollo, J. M. C.—*The New Eastern Europe: Western Responses*, Pinter Publishers for RIIA 1990.

Rollo, J. M. C. and Helen Wallace—New Patterns of Partnership in the New Europe Chapter 5 in '*The European Community and the Emerging Democracies of Eastern Europe*' a report by 6 European Institutes of International Relations, RIIA, 1991.

The Path of Reform in Eastern Europe, *European Economy*, Special Edition No. 2 1991.

Transition—Various Issues, The Newsletter about Reforming Economies, Socialist Economies Unit, The World Bank.

Wallace, Helen (ed)—*The Wider Western Europe* Pinter Publishing for RIIA (1991).

Notes

1 Throughout this paper Eastern Europe is defined as Bulgaria, Czechoslovakia, Hungary, Poland, Romania and Yugoslavia.
2 For a general discussion of these issues see Rollo et al., Granville & Rollo,
   CEPR, European, March and December 1990, as well as various editions
   of *Transition*.
3 For a fuller discussion see Wallace (ed.) and Rollo and Wallace.
4 Rollo et al. chapter 6.
5 See Pinder.
6 Printed in the House of Lords.
7 Collins & Rodrik.
8 Mr Benavides in evidence to the House of Lords Select Committee.
9 Source: Group of Thirty.
10 CEPR.

Financial Adaptation and the Optimal Timing of Financial Liberalization in Eastern Europe

SPECIAL MERIT AWARD

Summary

Political and economic reform, in addition to big monetary overhangs and big budget deficits make the prospect of extreme inflation in Eastern Europe almost certain if the proper steps are not taken in time. Financial adaptation will be unavoidable if these economies develop inflation. We discuss how this process generates strong feedback channels on inflation and exacerbates income distribution inequalities. The purpose of this essay is to use those arguments to support three basic ideas (i) monetary reform is the best alternative to the solution of the monetary overhang. (ii) monetary reform should be implemented as soon as possible. (iii) monetary reform should precede any attempt at financial liberalization. Only with stability and when price liberalization takes place can the financial sector carry on its role in the allocation of investment in the economy. A hasty and incorrectly phased financial liberalization may just help to trigger the economy into hyperinflation and create unnecessary income inequality.

Federico A. Sturzenegger is an Assistant Professor at the University of California, Los Angeles. An Argentine citizen he received his bachelor's degree from the Universidad Nacional de La Plata (1987) and his Ph.D. from the Massachusetts Institute of Technology (1991). Dr Sturzenegger's fields of research include the study of monetary instability and high inflation. His current research deals with understanding government policy in situations of extreme price instability and the implications of financial liberalization on growth.

7

Financial Adaptation and the Optimal Timing of Financial Liberalization in Eastern Europe

FEDERICO A. STURZENEGGER

1. Introduction

Financial adaptation: the shift of portfolios out of monetary holdings and into foreign currency, interest bearing assets, inventories or goods, is an unavoidable process in the presence of inflation and seigniorage financing.[1] Economists have long warned about the negative effects of inflationary financing such as: unexpected wealth transfers, the disruption of normal economic life, the use of an exaggerated amount of resources in the financial sector and excessive shopping. The most compelling reason for condemning inflationary financing though, is the strong regressivity of the inflation tax, a claim strongly supported empirically by low income elasticity of money demand. This essay shows that the existence of financial adaptation incorporates additional and stronger reasons to argue about the negative effects of inflationary financing. First, by reducing the base over which the inflation tax is levied, it strongly increases the rate of inflation and together with it, the distortion costs associated with inflation. Secondly, it affects income distribution by benefiting more strongly those individuals with higher income.

Latin America is a good sample to analyse in order to understand the implications of financial adaption. Many countries in the group have experienced high inflation for the last ten years, and the process of financial adaptation has gone far. During that period inflation has been increasingly higher and income distribution has systematically deteriorated. We look at Latin America today in order to understand Eastern Europe tomorrow: which with big monetary overhangs (an excess of real monetary balances over equilibrium levels), big budget deficits and increasing political pressures, the probability of extreme inflation is almost certain. Yugoslavia and Poland has already experienced instability, Bulgaria and the Soviet Union will probably be next.

There are two monetary problems in Eastern Europe today. First, a stock problem—the excess of real monetary balances, generated by years of printing money in an economy with effective price controls and no financial sector. While black markets are a part of everyday life, the amount of money held by agents is far above what they would be in a monetary equilibrium.[2] Second, a flow problem: the existence of large budget deficits which are financed through printing money.

Both problems have to be addressed if any solution to the inflation problem is to be found at all in the medium and long term. However this essay does not concentrate on the mechanisms for solving the deficit problem, but rather analyses the relative merits of the two alternatives for a solution of the overhang problem. A monetary overhang may be eliminated either through a liberalization of prices or through a radical monetary reform. The first choice will certainly generate inflation, which would then erode the level of real money balances to their equilibrium levels. Monetary reform comprises the reduction of nominal balances and was implemented by most European countries in the aftermath of World War II.

It is the intention of this essay to provide arguments for three basic ideas. (i) The relative benefits of monetary reform as a mechanism for reducing the monetary overhang. The inflationary solution may not only lead to hyperinflation but may strongly affect the pattern of income distribution along the way, generating undesirable income inequalities exactly as the economies move towards economic and political liberalization. (ii) The need for a quick implementation of such reform. Delayed stabilization in the presence of financial adaptation will only mean increasing inflation and instability in the economy. (iii) Financial liberalization should take place only after a solution to the overhang issue is more or less completed. If not, the financial sector, by providing alternative financial instruments, will be used as a mechanism for avoiding inflationary taxation and will probably enhance the possibility of extreme inflation with the negative consequences described in (i).

Table 1: Brazil and Argentina: Income Velocity and Ratio of Ml to M

	BRAZIL			ARGENTINA		
	M_1	M_4	M_1/M_4	M_1	M_3	M_1/M_3
1976	8.0	3.3	0.41	11.8	7.4	0.63
1980	11.9	4.4	0.37	14.0	4.5	0.30
1984	27.4	3.9	0.26	21.5	7.5	0.35
1988	33.3	3.8	0.11	24.4	6.0	0.25
1989	46.5	4.1	0.09	27.8	7.1	0.26

Source: Dornbusch et al., Extreme Inflations: Dynamics and Stabilization, *Brookings Papers*, 1990-2

Table 2: Argentina: % of Dollar Quotations

	10/3/91	3/1/90	26/10/90
Apartments	100%	100%	100%
Rents	77%	97%	86%
Cars	5%	98%	100%

Source: La Nacion, Buenos Aires, several issues.

2. The Effects of Dollarization

Financial adaptation has taken many forms; the development of indexed deposits, accumulation of commodities and foreign currency deposits. Table 1 shows the degree of financial adaptation experienced in Argentina and Brazil. If the financial system adapts then the velocity of M4 (or M3) should remain rather constant, while the velocity of Ml should increase substantially. Both economies show exactly that pattern indicating a strong degree of financial adaptation. In Brazil, for example, the development of checkable savings accounts has made the holding of currency almost unnecessary. In Argentina most of M3 are savings accounts, which allow five monthly extractions and which earn a rate slightly above expected inflation.

If the financial sector is not allowed to develop and adapt as in the above economies, the result will be an immediate dollarization of the economy, by this we mean the use of alternative means of payments to domestic currency: either dollars (or some other stable foreign currency) as in many Latin American countries or cigarettes as in the Soviet Union today.

An indication of the relative importance of dollarization is given in table 2. The table shows the percentage of transactions posted in US dollars in Argentina, for three selected dates and commodities. The first date is prior to the first hyperinflation which took place in mid 1989. The second column shows figures for a date in between the first and the second hyperinflation. Finally, the third column shows data for a date six months after the end of the second hyperinflation in March 1990. As can be seen in the table apartments have been a dollarized commodity throughout this period. The proportion of dollar quotations for rents seems to follow the rate of inflation while the car market, on the other hand, has experienced a complete dollarization following the first hyperinflation and most strikingly the market has remained dollarized even after inflation decreased.

Many times the government itself has provided the alternative currency. The Soviet government issued the Chervontsi in the 1920s as an indexed alternative to the Soviet Ruble.[3] The Hungarian government after World War II issued the Tax-pengo in order to index its tax revenues and later converted it into an indexed currency.[4] Nicaragua today has a similar monetary system with two currencies: the indexed Gold Córdoba and the depreciating New Córdoba. In Argentina, a multiple currency system existed for a brief period during the 80s, when individual states began issuing money in order to share in the collection of seigniorage, a source of revenue guaranteed by the constitution of the central government.[5] Eventually private monies may also arise; for example, during the German hyperinflation private issues of money amounted to about six times official currency.[6]

If inflation becomes pervasive, dollarization may be the next important issue of partial reform adjustment in Eastern Europe. Dollarization has two major effects on an economy which experiences moderate to high inflation, first, it increases the rate of inflation and second, it worsens income distribution.[7]

By reducing the base over which the inflation tax is collected, dollarization increases the equilibrium rate of inflation in the economy. It reduces the holdings of monetary balances because it provides both a more attractive alternative for saving and a more efficient transactions mechanism. It is also possible that the dollarization or the reduction in domestic monetary holdings may be big enough to make the level of government spending too large to be financed with taxes over the remaining money demand. In this case, hyperinflation will result before the government can react by adjusting the deficit. Of course, the likelihood of this occurring will depend on how easy it is to shift to an alternative currency or an alternative means of payments. Canada is an appropriate example of a country where this substitution can be done very quickly and easily. Because of the proximity to the US, the US dollar is already an accepted currency. If Canadian inflation were to get out of line, the response would be to shift quickly out of domestic currency and towards the US dollar, strongly curtailing any intent of seigniorage collection.

The second important and usually disregarded effect of dollarization is on income distribution. Dollarization affects different people in different ways because different goods are not bought in the same way and different people do not buy the same goods.

The first element to realize is that goods are purchased differently. When I go out for lunch or take a bus I pay with cash but when I go shopping and buy a compact disc or a shirt I use my credit card. If I buy a VCR or a car, I will probably write a cheque.

The second element to notice is that people buy different types of goods. Some individuals spend most of their income on necessities such as food, transportation and clothing. For others, the necessities are only a small fraction of their expenses, and most of their purchases are luxuries and durable goods.

Finally, it has to be recognized that necessities are usually purchased in small bundles while luxuries and durables usually comprise larger expenses. Financial adaptation develops in a way in which big transactions are favoured. The fixed fee for writing each cheque on our savings accounts only justifies its use for big purchases. The costs of running the credit card business usually imposes a minimum purchase requirement. When a foreign currency is held, usually only high denominations are available. In Latin America the holding of foreign currency includes only ten or higher denomination dollar bills and purchases below this level are automatically devoid of this means of transactions. With income levels of between 300 and 1000 dollars a year, daily spending averages between 1 and 3 dollars, and a majority of the population has no alternative but the local currency for transactions purposes. This situation has given rise to the expression of 'currency circuits', which illustrates the dichotomous means of payments structure: luxury goods operating in the dollar market and necessities with domestic currency.

In general the level of financial adaptation will provide savings for large purchases, and to some extent this is how it should be. The financial sector provides a service which has a similar cost for each transaction and therefore only large transactions should economically justify this cost. Unfortunately the process also increases the rate of inflation, and therefore the costs of holding domestic currency, which is the only available transaction resource for most of the population. The effect should by now be made clear, the poorest individuals have to use their holdings of domestic money for their purchases, paying a high inflation tax in the process. The richest on the other hand, use financial adaption as a vehicle for evading the inflation tax. This process therefore induces additional regressivity of inflationary financing.

3. What should be Done?

High budget deficits and monetary overhangs pose the most serious threat to price stability and therefore to a peaceful and softlanding transition to a market economic system for most East European countries. Pervasive inflation during the last ten years in Latin America has led to political instability, social conflict, a substantial deterioration of income distribution and a striking slow down in growth. There is a lesson to learn from those experiences which should be used to avoid the same mistakes in Eastern Europe.

Monetary systems are not uniquely shaped by the legal restrictions imposed by government. As was pointed out before there is an endogenous financial sector adaptation to inflation, which affects the macroeconomic equilibrium of the economy and affects income distribution. While it seems from above that financial adaptation may introduce harmful effects into the economy, to lay the blame on financial institutions would be like asking to close nuclear power plants *because* the government constructs atomic bombs. Financial institutions are key components of any market economy by channelling savings towards appropriate investment programs they solve one of the most important allocation problems any economy faces, fundamental for building an efficient production structure and attaining healthy growth.

The achievement of monetary equilibrium in Eastern Europe requires the solution to both the stock and the flow problems described above. Also, if these economies are to effectively transform to a market system at some stage both a price liberalization (to rationalize the allocation of production and consumption) and a financial sector liberalization (to rationalize the allocation of credit and capital) will have to be implemented.

The solution to the overhang problem in Eastern Europe requires either an economy-wide price liberalization, or a drastic monetary overhaul. The experience of the 1940s shows that price liberalization in the presence of excess monetary balances is a sure recipe for hyperinflation. As the price level jumps to its new higher level, changes in the pricing behaviour, erosion of real government revenues due to lags in the collection of taxes, and financial adaptation will all feed back and accelerate the inflationary process. It is needless to point out that hyperinflations are not cost-free experiences, and usually end with social unrest and political chaos. On the other hand, a radical monetary reform may be a more promising alternative. Different technical implementations tried during the late 40s in Europe suggest that a sizeable reduction in real monetary balances can be achieved with a reasonable probability of success.[8] The different alternatives include a currency conversion, as in the famed Erhardt's monetary reform of June 1948, which paved the way to the 'German Economic Miracle', or a blocking of financial assets, together with a posterior write-off or conversion into real assets, as in the cases of Belgium, Holland and Denmark. One of the most remarkable experiments in monetary reform was the Finnish monetary blocking of December 1945. All notes in denominations of over 100 Finmark were *cut in half*, the left half serving as legal tender at one-half the value of the original note. The right half was converted into a non-negotiable government bond to be redeemed by 1949.

While the sale of assets has been suggested as a way of reducing the monetary overhang and accelerating the process of privatization, an uncompromising write-off of currency, bank deposits and firms' debts appears to be a better alternative for future success of the reform. It would clean up the balance sheets of firms, providing the possibility of a fresh start for many productive activities, while the government could keep the resources provided by the future privatizations to implement a safety-net program, including temporary unemployment benefits, which would enhance the chances of a quicker and smoother conversion to a market system. W. Vocke[9] said in 1948 in support of the German monetary reform: '*Soft measures do not create hard currencies*', and policy makers should keep his words in mind. After the overhang problem is solved, prices should be liberalized, as with the risk of extreme inflation gone, one of the basic obstacles to price liberalization and therefore to the beginning of a rational economic system disappears. On this point we may add in Vocke's style: '*let prices increase, so that they may fall*'.

After solving the overhang problem, the flow issue of the budget deficit should be addressed if any long term success is actually going to take place in the fight for stability. Both Argentina in May and December 1989, and Brazil in March 1990 tried to curtail inflation by a write-off or blocking of monetary balances. Of course with no action taken on the budget side and an eroded confidence in the government, it did not take long before inflation returned. With deficits running above 9% of GNP both in 1988, 1989 and 1990, the Soviet Union faces a major challenge in this respect, and the solution to this problem will necessarily entail a reform of the tax system, elimination of many subsidies and probably a legal commitment to avoid further monetary financing of the treasury.[10] This is of course more easily said than done, and a detailed discussion of how this should be implemented clearly exceeds the purpose of this essay. While the solution to the budget deficit is essential, it will not come overnight. By contrast monetary reforms can usually be quickly implemented, and should forcefully be carried on. Delaying the solution may not only be reflected in positive and increasing inflation (with negative income distribution effects) but will also create uncertainty as to the future developments in the economy. Several monetary reforms during the 40s incorporated capital levies. The risk that this instrument may be once again used, may become an important hindrance to the inflow of capital and investment. This is what is happening today in Romania and Bulgaria and is the most likely scenario for the Soviet Union in the near future.

A key question in the short run is when should financial liberalization be implemented. More specifically, whether it should be carried on before the solution to the overhang problem (which, as argued above, should be followed by price liberalization) or afterwards.

Scenario 1: Financial liberalization prior to solution to overhang problem. A repressed financial system as still currently prevails in most of Eastern Europe may induce some of the informal channels of financial adaptation described above, with the negative implications discussed, i.e. increased pressure on the goods markets and incipient income distribution problems. A complete liberalization of the financial sector, without a prior solution to the overhang issue, may not only enhance the above effects, by adding additional mechanisms to avoid inflationary taxation for those with access to the financial sector, but may also be characterized by high real interest rates which people would demand in expectation of either a future write-off of monetary balances or a drastic increase in the price level. Needless to say, high interest rates, can become a serious hindrance to the recovery of activity and the development of new productive activities. In addition, government owned banks may suffer a banking crisis unless they also offer competitive interest rates, but with a portfolio of bad loans, the strain would eventually fall on the budget, inducing an even higher risk of instability. Of course, when price liberalization takes place, the existence of the financial sector will accelerate the inflationary process, providing alternative means of payments besides Ml and therefore making hyperinflation an even more threatening possibility. The final result of this strategy may well be an economy with unnecessary income inequality and devastated by hyperinflation.

Scenario 2: Solution to the overhang problem prior to financial liberalization. The description of the negative effects of the Scenario 1 is almost enough to suggest the relative benefits of the alternative phasing of reforms. After solving the overhang problem, hopefully through a write-off of nominal assets, prices can be liberalized without risk of extreme inflation. With inflation under control, financial liberalization should be strongly encouraged, and will generate none of the negative effects described above, but on the contrary, will be a key ingredient in channelling both domestic and international savings to the high productivity opportunities existing in these countries. With the recovery and stabilization, the prospect of a peaceful political and economic reform is improved.

4. Conclusions

Political and economic reform, in addition to the monetary overhangs and big budget deficits, make the prospect of extreme inflation in Eastern Europe almost certain if the proper steps are not taken in time. This essay discussed how the process of financial adaptation in an economy with inflation generates strong feedback channels on inflation and exacerbates income distribution inequalities. The purpose of this essay was to use those arguments to support three basic ideas: (i) Monetary reform is the best alternative to the solution of the monetary overhang. (ii) Monetary reform should be implemented as soon as possible. (iii) Monetary reform should precede any attempt at financial liberalization.

Only with stability and when price liberalization takes place can the financial sector carry on its role in the allocation of investment in the economy. On the contrary, it was shown that a hasty and incorrectly phased financial liberalization may just help to trigger the economy into hyperinflation and create unnecessary income inequality.

If Eastern Europe leaders want their countries, ten years from now, to look more like a typical Western European country rather than a typical Latin American country, they should learn from past economic experiences as history provides us with useful lessons. By showing the implications of persistent mistakes it makes us aware of the critical policy errors that should be avoided.

Notes

1 *Financial adaptation*: an optimal response of agents to escape inflation taxation should be distinguished from *financial liberalization*: a process of deregulation of credit and capital markets.
2 For an extensive discussion of the overhang problem see Dornbusch R. and Wolf H., (1990), *Monetary Overhang and Reforms in the 1940s*, NBER Working Paper No. 3456 and Leijonhufvud, Axel, *Inflation and Reform in the USSR*, Mimeo, UCLA.
3 See Katzenellenbaum, S. (1925), *Russian Currency and Banking 1914-1924*, London: PS King & Son, LTD and Yurovsky, L. (1925), *Currency Problems and Policy of the Soviet Union*, London: Leonard Parsons.
4 See Bomberg, W. A. and Makinen, G. (1983), 'The Hungarian Hyperinflation and Stabilization of 1945-1946, *Journal of Political Economy* Vol. 91, No. 51.
5 See Fernandez, R. (1991); 'What have Populists Learned from Hyperinflations?', in Sebastian Edwards and Rudiger Dornbusch (eds.), *Macroeconomic Policies and Income Distribution in Latin America*, University of Chicago Press.
6 See Keller, A. (1958), *Das Notgeld* Munich: Battenberg Verlag.
7 For a formal analysis see, Sturzenegger, F. (1991), *Inflation and Social Welfare in a Model with Endogenous Financial Adaptation*, Mimeo MIT.

8 For a complete description see Sherwin F. (1956), *Monetary Policy in Continental Europe: 1945-1952* University of Madison: Wisconsin Press.
9 First President of the Deutscher *Länder*, predecessor of the Bundesbank.
10 See Dornbusch R. and Wolf H. (1990), ibid.

Corporate Control and Financial Information

SPECIAL MERIT AWARD

Summary

This essay contrasts differences in financial intermediation structures between countries, focusing on the role of information in the relations between companies and financial intermediaries, in particular, banks. In defining a conceptual 'philosophy of finance', three factors in these relationships are considered: risk sharing, company control and contract enforcement. We note how business information is more 'public' but company-financial intermediary relationships less informationally and control interdependent in Anglo-Saxon countries than in Japan and continental Europe. Where banks are dominant in financial structures business information is generally less publicly available and companies more closely controlled; the reverse holds true where security markets are prevalent. The origins, advantages and problems of 'bank heavy' financial structures are compared with less intermediated structures.

The implication of our analysis is that the decline in the uniqueness of 'banks', the growth of non-bank intermediaries and the greater utilisation of financial markets by companies, particularly in the United States, will require greater central bank, regulatory and supervisory co-operation and attention to the maintenance of financial markets' functioning, liquidity and transparency.

In conclusion, the stability of financial institutions will not only be dependent on the 'protection' provided by government 'safety nets' but also in the supporting interrelationships and dependencies between firms and their sources of finance and control.

Joseph R. Bisignano is Assistant Manager, Monetary and Economic Department, Bank for International Settlements, in Basle, Switzerland. He received his Ph.D. in economics from Stanford University in 1971. Dr. Bisignano has taught at both Rutgers and Stanford Universities. From 1972 to 1985 he was associated with the Federal Reserve Bank of San Francisco, where he was Senior Vice President and Director of Economic Research before joining the BIS. His research areas have been primarily financial and monetary economics.

8

Corporate Control and Financial Information

JOSEPH R. BISIGNANO

Introduction

This essay argues that to understand the nature of recent changes in banking we need to consider the role that information plays in the relationships between business borrowers and financial intermediaries, and how differences in enterprise financial structures between countries are related to fundamental issues of risk-sharing, corporate control and contract enforcement. The intense competition in credit allocation between financial markets and financial institutions is also a competitive struggle between alternative information and corporate control systems. The issue is important because the nature of the interdependencies between companies and intermediaries which results from ongoing financial restructurings will alter the roles that central banks, financial regulators and supervisors play in ensuring the attain-ment of 'financial stability' and the costs to taxpayers when it is not achieved.

The Issue is Much More than that of 'Banking Structure'

It should not go without notice that the countries which have experienced the greatest deterioration in the strength of their banking systems during the 1980s also are those that have the most well-developed money and capital markets, primarily the Anglo-Saxon countries. The US Secretary of the Treasury, Nicholas Brady, recently stated, 'Today, the US does not have a single bank among the world's twenty-five largest. Twenty years ago we had seven'.[1] These same countries are also commonly credited with having the greatest public availability of information on the behaviour of firms. As a rule, the greater the role of the banking system as a source of business finance in an industrialised country, the less publicly available and more closely held is business information.

Joseph R. Bisignano

The OECD's 1990 information disclosure survey of 223 multi-national firms, entitled 'Survey on the Application of the Disclosure of Information Chapter of the OECD Guidelines' states:

In several areas such as sales, operating results, average number of employees and new capital investment, the reluctance of a considerable number of companies to provide segment information by line of business and/or geographical area is one of the main reasons why the results cannot be considered satisfactory and here the situation as compared to 1987 is virtually unchanged.[2]

Generally, the greater the role of banks as suppliers of business credit in the countries covered by the survey, the lower the compliance with the OECD information disclosure guidelines. The relationship is not spurious. The predominate position of banks in some countries also has implied a considerable amount of influence on the management of publicly traded corporations, compared with that exercised by non-bank equity holders. This 'corporate governance' role is even greater when a sizeable portion of the banking system is in the hands of the government, as in France and Italy. In others, where securities markets play a larger role in credit allocation, company information is less centrally controlled and more 'public'. Yet, it is not obvious that it is employed more efficiently. We are still searching, for example, for an understanding of the 1989 US equity market decline, which was supposedly triggered by little more than the failure to complete a leveraged buy-out. And considerable securities trading is said to take place solely on the basis of 'noise'.[3] These statements should not be taken as normative judgements. The comparative strengths of the banking industry and securities markets in the financial system depend on how these credit allocation structures utilise and safeguard information. The market for finance is inseparable from the market for information.

Publicly available information on companies is generally greater in Anglo-Saxon countries than in continental Europe or Japan. Hence, we see the use of 'central risk offices' in continental Europe, often lodged in the central bank, through which banks share information on large business borrowers. They do not exist in the United Kingdom or in the United States. Only recently have continental European and Japanese private credit rating firms emerged. 'Le rating est une technique et une pratique d'origine anglo-saxone'.[4] The modest public availability, close sharing and harbouring of information by firms is at the source of the greater reliance of continental European and Japanese companies on intermediated finance and for the greater use of debt in business financial structures. One reason for this differential financing behaviour is the difficulty and/or undesirability of company borrowers to *credibly* communicate in open financial markets valuable business information, yet they need to establish a credible 'signal' to their primary lenders. It also reflects means by which firms 'share risks' with financial intermediaries and, where banks are nationalised, with the government. Difficulties in 'information transfer' thus have promoted close debtor-lender relationships when the information from the firm could be more easily and safely transmitted to particular lenders and where the lender could 'test' its quality.

The pattern of closely held information also has contributed to closely held and managed companies, as is often observable in smaller European countries as a defence against takeover. The relationship between financial intermediaries, in particular banks, and companies sometimes meant that the creditor took a longer-term 'quasi-shareholder interest' in the firm, increasing with the level of credit extended. It also implied that at times bank financing considerably reduced the need for the firm to raise equity capital and compromise control. The modest bond issuance in some continental European countries arises from similar reasons, the desire to limit information availability when diffuse information and creditor structures might undermine the stability of the firm, either its source of finance, its performance or control.

Such arguments can be used to understand the historically greater use of bank finance and higher corporate leverage ratios in continental Europe and Japan and the significant differences in business information disclosure compared with the US and the UK. A look back at the 1966 EEC 'Segré Report' shows that in 1963 firms in Germany, France and Italy were all more highly leveraged than those in the UK and the US (Table 1). Referring to these three continental European countries the report states, '. . . the tendency for indebtedness to increase is gathering momentum: if this tendency were to continue, it would be cause for concern'.[5] Table 2 shows the continued predominant use of bank financing by non-financial companies in Japan and Germany and the overall modest reliance on open market paper. Although Japanese firms have begun to tap foreign bond markets heavily in recent years, overall securitised debt is still pale in comparison to bank debt. In contrast, bank financing is less in the United States and declining. These differences are in part attributable to the

Joseph R. Bisignano

Table 1 Financial structure of enterprises, 1963

	Ratio of realisable and liquid assets to short-term debts	Ratio of medium and long-term debt to cash flow	Ratio of medium and long-term debt to owners' equity
Germany	0.82	2.44	0.41
France	0.78	2.64	0.39
Italy	0.64	4.31	0.59
United Kingdom	1.05	n.a.	0.18
United States	1.31	1.50	0.24

Source: *The Development of a European Capital Market: Report of a Group of Experts appointed by the EEC Commission,* The Segré Report, European Economic Community Commission, Table 11, Brussels, November 1966.

desire in the former countries to maximise the value of 'private' information, where it could be guarded and risks shared among groups of interdependent firms and intermediaries. Such arguments also help to explain the greater use and tolerance in the past of informal and formal business cartels in Japan and continental Europe than in the United States. Some governments indeed have sanctioned cartels to promote economic stability where the economic and political costs of bankruptcy were high and where there was limited mobility of real factors of production and financial capital. In some countries banks aided the growth of industrial cartels. These arguments suggest that differences in company financial and banking structure among countries have part of their parentage in both the difficulty of the business sector in transmitting credible financial signals to an open market and the desire to harbour information which could be used to the disadvantage of the firm or a nation.

The financial cultural bias in Anglo-Saxon countries is for a wide dispersion of business information and corporate ownership claims and a competitive market in corporate control.[6] However, debt claimants often are discouraged by strong legal restrictions from taking active interest or control in the direction of the affairs of companies. The US legal doctrine of 'equitable subordination', for example, discourages major creditors from exercising significant influence over the borrowing company's decision-making for fear of reducing or losing their legal status as creditors in the event of bankruptcy; similarly with UK bankruptcy law.

Table 2 Total liabilities of non-financial companies[1]

	United States			Japan			Germany		
	1969	1979	1990	1969	1979	1990	1969	1979	1990
	As a percentage of total credit market liabilities								
1. Loans from financial institutions (2+3)[2]	53	47	42	95	94	85	91	95	95
2. Loans from banks[3]	31	27	25	55	50	56	85	86	83
3. Other loans[4]	22	20	17	40	44	29	6	9	12
long-term loans included in (1)[5]	*(18)*	*(14)*	*(6)*	*n.a.*	*n.a.*	*n.a.*	*(48)*	*(54)*	*(53)*
4. Short-term market paper	2	5	7	0	0	3	2	1	0
5. Bonds	45	48	51	5	6	12	7	4	5
6. Total credit market liabilities (1 + 4 + 5)	**100**	**100**	**100**	**100**	**100**	**100**	**100**	**100**	**100**

1 For Germany, producing enterprise sector.
2 For Japan, from domestic institutions only. In general, excludes securities.
3 For the United States, excludes mortgages.
4 Loans from non-bank financial institutions and government loans. For the United States and Canada, includes all mortgages. For the United States and Germany includes loans from banks located abroad.
5 For the United States, mortgages; for Germany, long-term bank loans.

Source: Country flow-of-funds statistics.

It is in Anglo-Saxon countries, primarily the United States, where we have recently observed the separation of corporate ownership from control contributing to a financial backlash: major equity retirements, the taking of firms private, an enormous rise in corporate indebtedness, a serious decline in corporate creditworthiness, on top of an increasing concentration of equity holding with institutional investors. In fact, the large rise in US enterprise indebtedness during the 1980s, much aided by the banking system, has made more difficult the legal distinction between debt and equity. The definition of equity as a fiduciary relationship and debt as a contractual relationship is increasingly undermined when debt takes on many of the risky characteristics of equity.[7] Corporate leverage ratios in the United States now have approached those in Japan and Germany, but with one difference. Much of the new US corporate debt is in marketable securities, while in the latter countries bank debt continues to dominate company balance sheets.

Changes in US corporate financial structure have gone hand-in-hand with a metamorphosis in banking. The current structural difficulties in the US banking industry are closely related to the competition from financial markets and foreign banks. The weakened competitive position of US banks can be appreciated by looking at the relative cost of equity capital, shown in Table 3. Sharp differences appear among countries; the cost of bank equity capital is much lower in 'bank dominated' financial systems. A similar picture is obtained in Chart 1, comparing bank stock price indices for the three major countries, together with an aggregate equity market price measure.

Structural problems also stem from US Government attempts to secure stability in an industry called 'banking' by excessively insuring, explicitly and implicitly, its liabilities, restricting competition and distancing the control relationships between business borrowers and certain classes of investors. As deregulation and competitive pressures mounted, the industry responded by substituting 'implicit capital', government deposit insurance, for costly equity capital.[8] As banks failed the US Government recognised that the true 'lender of last resort' was turning out to be the taxpayer. It recently has retreated on more than a half century of public policy by proposing legislation which would permit commercial ownership of 'new financial holding companies'.[9]

Table 3 Cost to bank equity capital (period average for 1984-90)

Country	Percentage
United States	11.9
Canada	10.3
United Kingdom	9.8
Germany	6.9
Switzerland	5.3
Japan	3.1

Source: S.A. Zimmer and R.N. McCauley, "Bank Cost of Capital and
International Competition", *Quarterly Review*, Federal Reserve Bank
of New York, Winter 1991.

At the other end of the financial spectrum, in an enviable sea of
banking stability and corporate solidity, lies Germany. Here banks
appear well capitalised and dominate as sources of business finance.
Money and capital markets are viewed by Anglo-Saxon critics as
'underdeveloped', and publicly available information on the performance of firms is modest by US standards. Why the difference?

During the nineteenth-century industrial development of Germany,
where investment was predominantly in heavy industry requiring
substantial amounts of long-term capital, German banks established
close long-term relations with firms, providing an early version of
'Allfinanz'. Banks took influential shareholder and management
positions in industry and, indeed, actively encouraged its cartelisation.
Today banks continue to play a prominent role on the boards of many
major German corporations and exercise sizeable proxy voting rights,
at times causing government and private concern over 'Die Macht der
Banken' (the power of banks).[10] There is very little of a corporate bond
market in Germany. The domestic bond market is dominated by the
government and banks. Most German company bond issuance, what
little there is, takes place offshore. Twenty-five years after the Segre
Report on the weakness of European capital markets, equity still is not
a major source of corporate financing. Even the Bundesbank has
pointed to 'narrowness and low capacity of the German share market'.[11] The cautious German attitude towards financial change is
illustrated in a recent speech by Deutsche Bundesbank president Karl
Otto Pöhl. Although quite a number of "financial market innovations",
. . . have not been introduced in the Federal Republic, or have only
been introduced more hesitantly than elsewhere, we can, in my view,

be quite satisfied with the development of our financial markets in the last few years'.[12]

Comparisons between US and German financial structures bring to mind the fable of the race between the tortoise and the hare. Tortoise Germany can be characterised as having a heavily intermediated financial system. Few businessmen bemoan the absence of a mature commercial paper market. Although German firms have ready access to international capital markets, most of their borrowing needs continue to be satisfied by domestic banks and other intermediaries. Financial claims on enterprises are not as heavily traded on secondary markets as in Tokyo, London or New York Only last January was the turnover tax on securities transactions removed. Looking at Germany, one wonders why anyone would think it necessary to create a capital market in Eastern Europe.

The hare financial system of the United States finds that over the 1980s domestic commercial banks have provided a sharply declining percentage of the external financial needs of the non-financial corporate sector (Table 4). The stock of banks' real estate loans is now greater than their commercial and industrial lending. Open markets, in particular the commercial paper market, have taken away many of the banks' better short-term credit customers and money market funds a sizeable proportion of their deposits. The bond markets, including the large private placement market, satisfy both intermediate and longer-term corporate needs. Central bankers now talk of banks having lost some of their 'franchise value', encouraging them to 'exploit the safety net' by engaging in riskier activities.

But there is much more than the intermediated structure of finance which differentiate countries' financial systems and something more fundamental; it depends on what might be termed 'the philosophy of finance'. This includes: (i) the content and the perceived merits of public disclosure of information on performance, ownership, financial structure and control of enterprises; (ii) the strength of belief in the allocative efficiency and stability of financial markets versus possibly less transparent financial institutions; (iii) the desired structure of and market for the ownership and control of companies, both non-financial and financial; (iv) perceptions of the existence of and the ability of public policy to exploit any trade-off between financial stability and efficiency in the allocation of capital; and (v) the culturally related structure of contract law and the required use of the courts to settle business contract disputes. And deep in the heart of the philosophy of

Chart 1

Stock markets: bank and general price indices

Weekly data - week ending 16-6-89 = 100

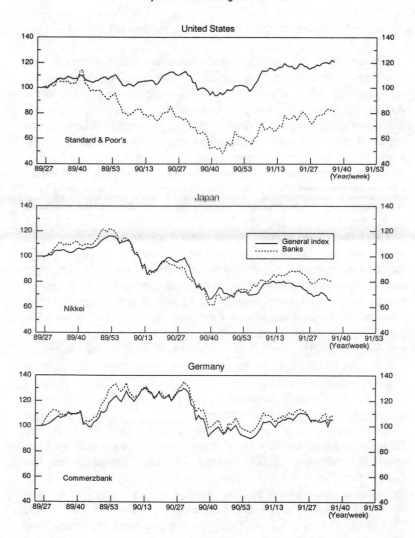

finance is the issue of how private enterprise financial activities should be governed; by an explicit rules-based system in open markets or 'internally' in institutions, through the use of less formal and less visible, long-term relationship contracts.

Enterprise Ownership and Control: Information is Control

Understanding comparative financial structures requires us to consider another economic abstraction, 'the firm'. What is it? Some suggest that it is simply a set of contracts used to manage and bear risks in the conduct of economic activity.[13] As such, it can be public or private. Both management and risk-bearing can be performed by suppliers of capital, shareholders and creditors, and by individuals hired to run the firm. Three problems are present in this characterisation. Firstly, contracts are often incomplete—they cannot incorporate all possible contingencies—and sometimes difficult to enforce without great cost. Indeed, the legal and market-related costs of contract dispute can be enormous. The battle between Texaco and Pennzoil over the takeover of Getty Oil, for example, is estimated to have reduced by almost $2 billion the total wealth of the two firms together.[14] Secondly, the different interests of the three groups need to be reconciled to minimise costly opportunistic behaviour. Japan and Germany are examples. Conflict resolution often appears to be obtained through informal 'club-like' business relations, information and risk-sharing and, importantly, outside of courts.[15] Witness the relative absence of 'hostile takeovers'. Thirdly, innovations in corporate finance and the increased use of debt make legal distinctions between debt and equity in some countries an important issue for the courts and especially for banks engaged in company takeover lending.[16] These issues relate to information and the control of the firm.

Ownership does not always imply control. In 1989 T. Boone Pickens Jr. found that even as the largest single shareholder of the Japanese automotive lighting manufacturer Koito Manufacturing Co. Ltd., with a 26% share in the firm, he could not secure three seats on the board of directors. Mr Pickens' attempt at board entry was blocked by Koito's appeal to its shareholders, including Toyota Motor Company. The rebuff should not have been a surprise. Individual Japanese shareholders typically play a very passive role as owners of firms. Washington's Japanese Economic Institute reports that in 1990 more than 1,600 publicly listed firms had their annual meeting on the same day, with the average meeting lasting less than thirty minutes.[17] Japan is not unique in this regard. In many other countries we find a weak relationship between the ownership and control of publicly traded companies. The European Community, for example, has not yet reached agreement on its 13th Company Law Directive dealing with takeovers. Some continental European countries do not think that all shares should have the same voting rights; those in favour, the British.

Restrictions on access to enterprise information and control should not be viewed simply as attempts by managers to protect their privileged positions. Instead, access to the firm implies entry into the set of formal and informal information and contract networks which govern its activities. Disturbances to these networks can upset its efficiency and stability. Restricting access to company information is common in all countries for simple competitive reasons—examples: to discourage entry or takeover, to protect property rights, and to attempt to secure returns on long-term investments. Financial firms quite reasonably play an important role in this regard. To quote a money manager in a recent *Wall Street Journal* article, 'I think it's important that the Dutch financial industry hold hands to help shield Dutch firms from foreign predators'.[18]

The 'hand holding' by financial intermediaries of client non-financial companies, for reasons of risk-sharing, takeover protection and, importantly, for stabilising profits and longterm investment, is best illustrated with the example of the Japanese corporate 'keiretsu' groupings. These business groups have been accused by some Americans as presenting trade barriers. Under the Japan-US Structural Impediments Initiative the Japan Fair Trade Commission is to investigate transactions among keiretsu firms to see if they 'impede fair competition'.[19]

Not surprisingly, six of the large Japanese keiretsus are centred on a 'main bank'. All are in part a response to Japan's Antimonopoly Law which prohibits a holding company corporate structure. The essential characteristic of these informal groupings, which can include a large bank, insurance company, securities firm, trading company, manufacturers, suppliers and retailers, is that of risk- and information-sharing. This is obtained by the extensive use of cross-equity holdings, overlapping boards of directors, personnel exchanges and frequent meeting of group members. Keiretsu-related companies continue to rely on bank finance, but with recent heavy use of bond market finance, primarily foreign. They seem not to benefit from close business relationships in terms of higher profits, but more stable returns and greater long-term investment than their foreign competitors. To some, these informal relationships appear anti-competitive and the information structure 'closed' to outsiders. To others, who stress economic stability, the groupings appear as an efficient way to share business risks, reduce adjustment costs to changes in non-diversifiable macroeconomic risk and minimise the expense of resolving business disputes.

The Anglo-Saxon bias is for 'open' business information and corporate control systems and frequent economic 're-contracting' (renegotiation of formal contracts). The adjective 'open' is meant to indicate both the degree to which financial claims on the firm are traded in secondary markets and the ease, cost and extent to which information on the prospects, past performance and the economic structure of companies is available to investors. The presumption is that the greater the availability of information to financial markets and the more frequent the trading of financial claims the greater will be the efficiency in the valuation of firms.

The second half of the 1980s has dented the optimism of many market efficiency enthusiasts. Indeed, US corporate financial activity during this period can be interpreted as the result of certain large investors having taken seriously the empirical evidence developed by academics during the 1970s on the market valuation of US corporations. These studies often indicated that the equity market appeared to seriously undervalue the net worth of US non-financial corporations. Believing this evidence one might have been led to act as did leveraged buy-out specialists—retire the equity and sell pieces of the firm to reduce the debt used to take it over.

While one may be taken aback by the enormous growth of risky, low-quality US corporate debt, one should not lose sight of the message: there were serious information and control problems which prevented US firms from being properly valued. The result found the financial structures of many US firms moving closer to that of their continental European and Japanese competitors, meaning more debt and less equity. Similarly, a greater number of US companies are now more closely managed and controlled, again, like many company governance relationships in Europe and Japan. Yet the trend towards convergence among industrial countries in the leverage of non-financial companies does not entail the same relationship between corporate borrowers and suppliers of credit. There has been an increasing displacement of US banks by securities markets in the financing of enterprises.

Financial Stability in a World of Reduced Commercial Bank Intermediation

The attainment of macro-financial stability depends on the role that financial intermediaries, bondholders and shareholders play in monitoring firms and on the transferability and credibility of business information. Yet monitoring by itself is insufficient to guarantee prudent borrower behaviour. Claimants, be they shareholders or lenders, should be able to exercise some form of influence on corporate managers, other than through their ability to simply sell their shares and bonds or refuse to grant further credit. Restrictions on institutional investor behaviour, however, have reduced the number of 'active investors' in the US, creating a corporate 'prisoner's dilemma' by limiting the ability of different claimants and the firm to 'co-operate' and share risks and information.[20] These problems are made more difficult by the increased use of securitised finance and the diminished role of banks as suppliers of business credit.

There are several ways in which company information and control problems may be reduced. The choice depends on normative judgements of the factors described above defining the 'philosophy of finance'. One is to require increased disclosure of information on publicly traded corporations. The UK Accounting Standards Board has recently proposed a radical change in company accounting rules, more in common with US GAAP standards.[21] Reform might also be sought by promoting a competitive market in corporate control. In the US and UK, for example, regulations regarding corporate takeovers could be relaxed.[22] Alternatively, banking-corporate structures could be promoted which ensure claimants a role in influencing company behaviour and foster a greater sharing of information among enterprises. In France we are seeing a renaissance of bank activities resembling those of the *démodé* 'banques d'affaires', namely the purchase of corporate shares.[23] An old debate returns with all of these alternatives: how close or distant ought to be the relationships between 'banks' and industry in order to maximise the returns from private information? For it is on the efficiency in the allocation and use of business information by financial markets and intermediaries which financial stability ultimately depends.

Notes and References

1 'Last Chance for a Sweeping Overhaul', *Financial Times*, 4th April 1991.
2 Organisation for Economic Co-operation and Development, Working Document by the Working Group on Accounting Standards, No. 6, 'Survey on the Application of the Disclosure of Information Chapter of the OECD Guidelines', 1990, page 8, Paris.
3 Fischer Black, 'Noise', *Journal of Finance*, 1986.
4 François Daulon, 'Actualité de la notation', *Revue d'Economie Financière*, Printemps/Eté 1990, page 1.
5 'The Development of a European Capital Market: Report of a Group of Experts appointed by the EEC Commission', European Economic Community Commission, page 63, Brussels, November 1966.
6 The market-oriented view of the transfer of corporate control can be seen in economist-lawyer Richard A. Posner's book *Economic Analysis of Law*, Third Edition, Little, Brown and Company, 1986.
7 Robert E. Scott, 'Discussion', in 'Are the Distinctions between Debt and Equity Disappearing?', Federal Reserve Bank of Boston, Conference Series No. 33, October 1989.
8 One of the first to point this out was S. Pelzmann in, 'Capital Investment in Commercial Banking and its Relationship to Portfolio Regulation', *Journal of Political Economy*, 1970.
9 'Modernising the Financial System: Recommendations for Safer, More Competitive Banks', The Department of the Treasury, Washington DC, February 1991.
10 'Zur Diskussion um die Macht der Banken', Bundesverband Deutscher Banken, September 1989.
11 Report on the Deutsche Bundesbank for the year 1981, page 22.
12 Speech by President of the Deutsche Bundesbank, Karl Otto Pöhl, at the Frankfurt Stock Exchange, Frankfurt am Main, 21st March 1991.
13 Eugene F. Fama, 'Agency Problems and the Theory of the Firm'. *Journal of Political Economy*, 1980.
14 P. McCutler and L. H. Summers. 'The Costs of Conflict Resolution and Financial Distress: Evidence from the Texaco-Pennzoil Litigation', National Bureau of Economic Research, Inc., Working Paper No. 2418, October 1987.
15 For a discussion of how 'internal organisation' in certain circumstances has advantages over 'market contracting' see Oliver E. Williamson, *Markets*

and Hierarchies Analysis and Antitrust Implications, A Study of the Economics of Internal Organisation, The Free Press, 1975.

16 A. De Natale and P. B. Agram, 'The Doctrine of Equitable Subordination as Applied to Nonmanagement Creditors', *The Business Lawyer*, February 1985.

17 'Patterns and Implications of Japanese Stockholding', JEI Report Japan Economic Institute, Washington DC, 25th January 1991.

18 'ABP Ponders Greater Public Role After Dutch Takeover Barriers Fall', *Wall Street Journal*, 26th March 1991.

19 Dick K. Nanto, 'Japan's Industrial Groups, The Keiretsu', in Japan's Economic Challenge, Joint Economic Committee, Congress of the United States, October 1990.

20 See Mark J. Roe, 'Political and Legal Restraints on Ownership and Control of Public Companies', *Journal of Financial Economics*, 1990.

21 'UK Seeks Clearer Company Accounts', *Financial Times*, 11th April 1991.

22 The case for a relaxation of UK restrictions on takeover activity is argued by Mervyn King and Ailsa Roell, 'The Regulation of Takeovers and the Stock Market', *National Westminster Bank Quarterly Review*, February 1988.

23 See Madlyn Resener, 'Haus banks à la française', *Institutional Investor*, December 1990 and Federico Rampini, 'Si moltiplicano in Francia gli accordi tra banche, imprese e assicurazzioni', *Bancaria*, January 1990.

Information Technology, Trade in Financial Services and Evolving Regulatory Priorities

SPECIAL MERIT AWARD

Summary
The application of information technology (IT) has greatly augmented the tradability of financial services. Ongoing changes in IT and regulatory regimes imply that financial institutions will face fewer constraints than ever before in serving foreign markets. As a result, both cross-border trade in financial services and physical establishment in foreign markets are likely to increase, the former stimulated in part by increased competition between national financial centres, the latter driven by a desire to sell products at the retail level. The complexity and high cost of up-to-date IT applications is inducing firms to specialize, with many pursuing outsourcing and niche strategies. An implication of this is that cross-border trade in information-intensive intermediate inputs will become more important for financial service providers. The increasing IT-intensity of financial activity in both wholesale and retail markets alters the relative importance and sectoral focus of the regulatory issues that should be of primary concern to the industry. In particular, when attempting to reduce regulatory impediments to international competition, financial institutions should devote greater attention to the input side. This includes the conditions of access to—and use of—telecommunications networks and the reliability of the electronic infrastructures, both of which are central to the continued internationalization of financial markets.

Bernard M. Hoekman is an economist in the Economic Research and Analysis Unit of the General Agreement on Tariffs and Trade, Geneva, Switzerland. A graduate of Erasmus University Rotterdam, he received his Ph.D. in economics from the University of Michigan (1988). His research interests include the theory and practice of commercial policy, the role of services-related trade and foreign direct investment and multilateral co-operation. He has published numerous articles on these subjects in books and professional journals such as *Canadian Journal of Economics, Kyklos, The World Economy*, and *International Organization*. In 1990 he received a Special Merit Award in *The AMEX Bank Review* competition for the essay 'Contingent Commercial Policies and the Credibility of Financial Market Liberalization' written with Michael P. Leidy.

Pierre Sauvé is Assistant Services Negotiator in the Canadian Department of External Affairs and International Trade's Office of North American Free Trade Negotiations. He is a former staff member of the General Agreement on Tariffs and Trade, in Geneva, and of the Bank for International Settlements, in Basle. He received his postgraduate training in economics at Cambridge and Oxford Universities.

9

Information Technology, Trade in Financial Services and Evolving Regulatory Priorities

BERNARD M. HOEKMAN AND PIERRE SAUVÉ

I. Introduction

Technological advances in telecommunications, information processing and computing are universally agreed to have been a major factor underlying the growth of financial innovation and the corresponding surge in cross-border activity witnessed during the last fifteen years. Such developments show few signs of abating. It is widely expected, indeed, that technological innovation will, alongside the forces of deregulation, competition and liberalisation, play a major role in sorting out leaders from laggards in the world's financial markets during the coming decade.

Ongoing changes in information technology (IT)[1] and increasingly convergent regulatory regimes imply that financial institutions will face fewer constraints than ever before in serving foreign markets. This essay looks at two issues that arise in this context: first, the impact IT will have on international trade in financial services (at both the wholesale and retail levels); and second, the implications of the ever increasing IT-intensity of the financial production process for corporate attitudes towards the process of regulatory reform in both the financial and telecommunications sectors.

II. IT and the Internationalization of Financial Markets

The conventional wisdom in financial circles during much of the 1980s was that international liberalisation, technological advances and the further integration of international capital markets would lead to the emergence of a small group of super banks/financial supermarkets spanning the globe.[2] For a number of the world's leading financial institutions, the urge to 'go global' did prove irresistible. This set in motion a process whose main features are by now familiar: a frenzy of mergers and acquisitions activity, particularly in the securities business, a proliferation of new entrants in all major financial centres and market segments, strong growth in spending on IT (outlays by US commercial banks alone representing some $15 billion in 1990), relentless price competition in wholesale markets, and increasing competition at the retail level in national markets as a result of (the threat of) establishment by foreign-owned firms.

Internationalization of Wholesale Markets

It is at the wholesale level that the effects of IT have been most vividly felt, increasing both the tradability of financial services and the volume of cross-border trade in numerous financial instruments. Indeed, for a number of wholesale market segments—such as foreign exchange, securitized credits, derivative products—large scale international arbitrage has caused markets to become increasingly integrated across national financial centres. This in turn has provided a strong stimulus to regulatory reform. As a result, firms engaged in the provision of wholesale products have seen their theatre become increasingly global in scope as regulatory obstacles have receded.

IT has played a dual role in this connection. First, it has allowed sizeable economies of scale to be reaped. Second, the lowering of spreads and profit margins resulting from increasing competition worldwide has induced—indeed forced—financial service providers to continuously invest in new IT and develop new IT intensive products to maintain a competitive edge. IT has therefore led to both greater trade in 'standard' financial products (foreign exchange, securities) and *created* international markets for new products (derivatives, securitised loans, etc). Cross-border trade in equity as a percentage of total world stock turnover more than doubled between 1979 and 1989, to over 14 per cent. On Europe's equity markets one in every three transactions now involves a foreign investor. At year-end 1989, trading by non-residents in US government securities reached $3 trillion, or roughly $12 billion per day. Non-residents account for over one-third of the value of all transactions in German bond markets. The growing integration (and physical interconnection) of securities markets worldwide and the advent of round-the-clock trading has in turn spurred the creation and rapid growth of cross-border trade in derivative products.

For instance, futures contract trading on Eurodollar interest rates increased almost 55 per cent annually since the mid-1980s, reaching close to 47 million in 1989. Moreover, combining futures and options, more than 40 million contracts on various foreign currencies were traded worldwide in 1989, up from 14 million in 1983.[3]

In a growing number of markets, the internationalization process shows signs of having come full circle, with banks and other financial institutions now rediscovering the many virtues of traditional domestic markets. By driving home the need to revamp inefficient and often highly segmented domestic financial markets, one of the major, if somewhat paradoxical, effects of international liberalization has been to promote the gradual return of markets and financial institutions to the domestic base from the liberal 'offshore' centres to which they had initially migrated. The explanation for this holds in two words: regulatory convergence, a trend which over the past decade has seen the world's financial markets regulated in increasingly homogenous ways at the domestic level and subjected to supervisory standards and regulatory practices at the international level that are becoming increasingly (albeit unevenly) harmonised.

The trend towards greater dependence of financial institutions on domestic markets owes much to the recent campaign of supervisory authorities throughout the world to strengthen banks' balance sheets and capital ratios. By raising the cost of capital to banks, the Basle agreement on capital adequacy[4] has provoked far-reaching changes in corporate strategies, prompting many financial institutions, many of which had spread themselves thin in trying to become global players, to focus on domestic activities as a prime source of capital growth. Moves in this direction have been fuelled as well by the advent in Europe of a continent-wide market for financial services by the end of 1992 and by the gradual erosion in a number of established and emerging financial markets of barriers to entry and to geographic expansion within domestic markets (US, Japan, Canada, Republic of Korea, etc.).

The main consequence of the trend towards reverse migration is that the 'international' market for financial services is becoming less and less an offshore one. It is, instead, being transformed into one in which domestic markets are plugged in internationally. Frequently this is accompanied by greater specialization in the provision of a limited set of services, i.e., the pursuit of niche strategies. This has important implications for the role of IT and cross-border transactions in the corporate mission of financial institutions. For one, spending on—and mastering of—IT will condition the ability of financial institutions to reduce their costs, add value to and differentiate their products. IT will, at the same time, be a key ingredient in the competitive battle that will be fought *between* liberal national financial markets (as opposed to *within* liberal offshore markets), the main reason being that such a battle will be fought over globe-spanning trading networks.

Indeed, it is widely expected that just as the 1980s saw a proliferation of competing firms, so the 1990s will see a proliferation of competing trading networks. This has already become a reality in the world's foreign exchange and derivatives market as well as in the market for information services. For example, the Chicago Mercantile Exchange (CME), the Chicago Board Options Exchange (CBOE), the London International Financial Futures Exchange (LIFFE), the London Futures and Options Exchange as well as Frankfurt's Deutsche Terminborse have all recently unveiled new computer networks which bypass trading floors. Reuters' Dealing 2000 system allows foreign exchange traders around the world not only to enter orders and match them automatically but to provide an instantaneous record of the price at which transactions are proposed and made. Just as opening up financial centres did in the 1980s, by opening up new markets to new participants, trading networks will in the 1990s help to increase international trade in financial services. Such trade will be ever more IT-intensive, as IT acts as both the delivery vehicle and constitutes a significant part of total value-added.

Internationalization of Retail Markets

It has not so far led to a marked increase in cross-border trade in retail banking services, even though improvements in IT have already significantly increased the *tradability* of financial services at the retail level, and will continue to do so in the future. Technically, it is quite feasible for a bank to establish automatic teller machines (ATMs) in a number of countries (as illustrated by American Express's ubiquitous cash dispensing machines) through which it can offer its financial services. Or, banks may consider the pursuit of a 'home banking' strategy, providing (foreign) customers with communications software and a modem so as to allow them to use their personal computers to access the bank's central computing system. However, to the extent that cross-border trade occurs, it still consists mainly of transactions associated with business travel and tourism, e.g. credit card transactions and limited accessing of ATMs when abroad. In part this is due to regulatory restrictions affecting the cross-border delivery of retail products. Arguably, however, even in a world of complete convergence of regulatory regimes for retail activities, cross-border trade in financial services would be relatively minor.

Although IT greatly lowers processing and transaction costs, financial institutions will typically need to maintain a physical presence in different national markets in order to provide retail services most efficiently. Even if it is the case that the costs of providing cross-border financial services are sufficiently low to be price-competitive with domestic firms, other costs—greater uncertainty, lesser name recognition, perceived problems of security, limited geographical coverage of the electronic network, prudential 'muddling' on the part of host country supervisory authorities, etc.—are likely to remain high enough to discourage many potential retail clients from doing a substantial part of their banking with financial institutions located abroad. Moreover, frequently the costs associated with setting up, running and using the electronic infrastructure will be high, for both consumers and providers of the service. The advantages of having access to a local branch network and of being able to interact with financial service providers on a face-to-face basis will prove very difficult to overcome via IT applications alone.

Rather than pursuing cross-border trading opportunities, financial institutions that have developed a competitive advantage in the provision of specific retail products can be expected to continue to establish a physical presence in foreign markets that are of interest to them. This may imply building up a local branch network—either from scratch or via acquisitions or mergers—and becoming a full service provider. Alternatively, capital constraints may encourage financial firms to pursue niche strategies or joint ventures in foreign markets. The broad direction of regulatory reform in developed country markets, enshrined in the OECD's Codes of Liberalization of Capital Movements and Current Invisible Operations, as well as its National Treatment instrument, has been to significantly increase the contestability of financial markets. Thus, their product coverage has expanded and requirements that non-resident enterprises be permitted to establish in host countries and be treated in the same manner as domestic firms have been strengthened.[5] In further facilitating the ability of financial service providers to operate in foreign markets, the advent of plurilateral (EC-92) and multilateral (BIS, OECD, Uruguay Round) disciplines will improve competitive conditions further. As a result, retail banking may become a truly global business for the first time in its history. However, investment, as opposed to trade, will be the vehicle for this.

While changes in regulatory regimes are, of course, an important element in the process of internationalization, IT will tend to be the driving force. Frequently, an IT capability with associated economies of scale or scope that was developed for other (usually home) markets is the source of a foreign firm's competitive advantage over domestic incumbents, and thus the decision to enter a market. Cross-border flows of information and IT-intensive ancillary services (mostly intermediate inputs) associated with financial activities at the retail level will become ever more crucial determinants of the competitiveness of financial firms in retail markets. This will hold for domestic firms as well as foreign affiliates, but perhaps more so for the latter, given the need for international telecommunications links to access parent company information systems and obtain 'headquarter services'.

More generally, the high costs of keeping up with IT developments can be expected to lead to an increase in outsourcing of specific applications such as data processing, software development, network management, and back-office activities, a trend that has already engulfed today's wholesale markets. An increasing number of firms are either contracting certain back-office activities to third parties, or specializing in such services. For example, a significant share of all US credit card transactions are processed by specialized firms. Third-party vendors offer various types of computing services, ranging from maintenance and software support to the management or provision of IT facilities or networks. Another area where financial firms are contracting out is for custody services: managing the payment and settlement of transactions, collecting dividends and interest, safe-keeping, tax reclamation and related bookkeeping services. Global custody operations in particular are very IT-intensive, speed and accuracy of processing being the key to providing custody services successfully. Many financial institutions have decided to leave this market segment to specialized firms, who also offer custody-related, IT-intensive products such as data analysis, securities lending, performance measurement, valuation reporting, as well as full master trust reporting services through which settlement and reporting functions are consolidated.[6] As the physical location of firms offering such services is irrelevant, this is likely to lead to more international transactions.

Summing up, the application of IT is central to the internationalization of financial markets, at both the wholesale and retail levels. At the wholesale level IT is a key ingredient of the financial production process. Moreover, it constitutes the backbone of the trading networks that allow cross-border transactions to occur, the volume of which is set to increase further as financial institutions return to national financial centres. At the retail level IT is frequently the source of competitive advantage that induces financial firms to establish a presence in multiple markets. The complexity and high cost of up-to-date IT applications is inducing firms to specialize, with many pursuing outsourcing and niche strategies. As a result, cross-border trade in intermediate inputs—various types of information—can be expected to become an increasingly important factor stimulating further internationalization of financial markets.

III. Implications for Regulatory Priorities

In confronting the set of new competitive conditions prevailing in the world's financial markets, banks and other financial institutions face two main challenges. A first challenge stems from the need to simultaneously reduce costs, improve/increase IT-driven product ranges, and raise the amounts of capital that will be necessary to play in global finance's major leagues. A second challenge concerns the need to secure access to the widest possible market base over which to defray growing operating costs, a major component of which is IT-related. In meeting both challenges, financial service providers can be expected to continue to expend considerable resources in convincing national authorities of the need to maintain the pace of regulatory reform achieved in recent years. As large-scale users of telecommunications services, financial institutions have also acquired a major stake in the liberalization of domestic and international regulatory environments in the telecommunications sector. In both regards, the central need of banks and other financial institutions is to be confronted by regulatory environments that are fair, i.e. non-discriminatory, predictable, i.e. transparent, and liberal, i.e. competition-inducing.

130   *Bernard M. Hoekman and Pierre Sauvé*

The trend towards increasingly liberal regulation of financial activities—particularly in developed country markets, but also in a growing subset of emerging markets—while by no means complete, is relatively advanced. Developments such as reverse migration of financial institutions to home markets, the emergence of competing trading networks and 24-hour screen-based trading, as well as increasing foreign direct investment to service retail markets imply that in the 1990s the primary public service policy issue for the financial industry may well relate to the operation and availability of domestic and international electronic infrastructures and information networks than to issues of financial regulation *per se*.

There are two aspects to this. The first relates to the costs and conditions under which firms can secure access to—and use—a varied menu of telecommunications transport services. The second relates to the security and reliability of trading and information networks.

The requirements of financial institutions for telecommunications facilities and services vary greatly, depending on their size, specialization, centralization, etc. There are, nonetheless, a number of user needs which many, if not most, internationally active financial institutions share. Financial institutions make heavy and increasing use of both basic telecommunications services and so-called value-added network services (VANs) and other enhanced information services. A first need is to be unconstrained regarding the choice of basic telecommunication services and to be able to use such services without arbitrary restrictions.[7]

Another important telecom issue affecting the financial services industry relates to tariffs. To contain telecommunications costs, national and international regulatory bodies must be induced to reduce rates and to move away from the volume-sensitive pricing of leased circuits. Furthermore, users should have flexibility in choosing equipment and attaching it to public or private networks. Freedom to choose customer premises equipment provides firms with a highly prized marketing tool, allowing them to differentiate their products and services from those of competitors. Restrictions affecting the choice of equipment can limit a country's nationals from benefiting from foreign innovations and oblige service providers to accept sub-optimal networking and marketing strategies. A closely related issue is that of standardization. Standards in the IT field offer users considerable benefits in connectability and cost, but may also be used to stifle competition. Standards (and standards-setting processes) should be internationally agreed, simple, and transparent. The financial sector has a substantial interest in promoting the development and adoption of 'open network architectures' and in insisting that the attachment of terminal equipment to public networks be subject to a minimalist 'no harm to the network/network personnel' standard.

In addition to telecommunications-related regulatory issues, there is a need to establish appropriate safeguards to ensure that electronic trading and information networks are secure and reliable. In this connection the primary issue relates to payments and settlements. If clearing of international transactions is subject to more than minimal risk—for example, if there is a chance of significant delay in settlement—this can be extremely costly and inhibit the use of electronic trading. A recent Group of Thirty paper[8] has recommended that moves be pursued to shift to 'paperless' settlement as quickly as possible, this being a necessary condition for timely clearing of transactions. IT will be central to any effort aimed at creating a dematerialized settlements environment, the basic element being computer-driven centralized securities depositories that allow transactions to be processed in book entry form. Space constraints prohibit a detailed discussion of the issues involved, which require cooperation between financial institutions. However, they are primarily technical and should therefore in principle be relatively straightforward to settle.

IV. Conclusions

Changes in the technological direction of financial institutions will be required to face the coming decade's increasingly competitive environment. For many financial institutions, this will involve an IT orientation characterized both by efficiency-enhancement in regard to transactional and operational capabilities and by upgraded delivery capabilities in regard to information-based services. This can be expected to fuel continued (if more selective) spending on new technology and applications, lead to their wider dispersion within firms and among end-users, increase the need for improvements in banking infrastructures worldwide, and place an ever-greater emphasis on security and reliability. Most importantly, the continued internationalization of financial service activities vastly expands the need for flexible, readily accessible and competitively-priced telecommunications services at both the national and international levels.

Cross-border trade in wholesale financial services is likely to continue its rapid expansion during the 1990s. In part this will be driven by recent regulatory reforms, which has induced a move away from offshore activities towards domestic markets. As a result, national financial centres will compete increasingly with one another for international wholesale business. Furthermore, IT may have a strong widening effect in wholesale markets by allowing an expanded range of new (albeit 'tested') financial products and processes to be introduced in a large and expanding number of emerging markets, such as the countries of Eastern and Central Europe and the coming decade's newly industrialized countries. Retail markets are unlikely for their part to be a major growth area in cross border trade. Rather, the economics of the industry dictates that financial firms will need to continue to require a physical presence in order to compete in foreign markets. Nonetheless, cross-border flows of information associated with the provision of retail financial services will continue to expand, in part due to specialization and unbundling fuelled by the spiralling costs associated with keeping up with IT developments. Indeed, the growth in cross-border trade in intermediate *inputs* may expand as much as international trade in financial service *outputs*.

The policy implication of the increasing IT-intensity of financial production and trade is that it alters the relative importance and sectoral focus of the regulatory issues that should be of primary concern to the industry. Thus, when attempting to achieve a further reduction in regulatory impediments to international competition, greater attention needs to be devoted to the intermediate input/ infrastructure side. Indeed, if the recent trend towards regulatory convergence is maintained, restrictions on the contestability of financial markets may well come to be embodied in technical requirements that prohibit the use of new or least-cost technologies or equipment. There may be a parallel with merchandise trade liberalization, where technical barriers to trade such as standards have been much more difficult to eradicate than direct barriers such as tariffs.[9] This is not to say that financial regulations will not continue to limit international competition. After all, import-competing firms will generally have an incentive to seek to restrict foreign competition.[10] At a minimum, however, the agenda needs to be broadened.

While progress has been made in recent years in liberating the telecommunications sector from antiquated market structures and regulatory practices, much remains to be done. Relative to the trend of financial market liberalization, which shows no signs of being reversed, changes in the telecommunications area have been slow and uneven across countries. As major users of telecommunications services, more than the current small minority of financial institutions will need to make their voices heard in order to ensure that *non-financial* regulations will not come to restrict further internationalization and integration of financial markets.

References

Baer, Herbert and Douglas Evanoff, 1990, 'Payments System Issues in Financial Markets That Never Sleep', *Economic Perspectives*. Federal Reserve Bank of Chicago, November.

Bank for International Settlements, 1991, *61st Annual Report*, Basle: BIS.

Dixon, Hugo, 1990, 'Why the open skies stay closed,' *Financial Times*, July 17.

Group of Thirty, 1989, *Clearance and Settlement Systems in the World's Securities Markets*, New York, March.

Hoekman, Bernard and Michael Leidy, 1991, 'Contingent Commercial Policy and the Credibility of Financial Market Liberalization', in Sarah Hewin and Richard O'Brien (eds.), *Finance and the International Economy: 4*, Oxford: Oxford University Press.

Hoekman, Bernard and Pierre Sauvé, 1991, 'Integration and Interdependence: Information Technology and the Transformation of Financial Markets', mimeo.

Ley, Robert, 1989, 'Liberating Capital Movements: A New OECD Commitment', *The OECD Observer*, 159 (August-September), 22-26.

Notes

1 IT comprises the integration of computing and telecommunications hardware and software, allowing large volumes of information to be collected, processed and exchanged reliably and rapidly.

2 This section draws on Hoekman and Sauvé (1991).

3 Baer and Evanoff (1990), Hoekman and Sauvé (1991).

4 The Basle agreement on international convergence of capital measurement and capital standards, completed in July 1988, requires banks to have so-called tier 1 capital-equity and retained earnings equal to 4 per cent of assets, and total capital equal to 8 per cent of assets by the end of 1992. See e.g. BIS (1991).

5 See Ley (1989) for a discussion of the contents of—and recent changes to—the OECD instruments.

6 Hoekman and Sauvé, 1991.

7 E.g. being permitted to share and/or re-sell unwanted leased-circuit capacity and to process, store and transmit their information (voice, data, text, facsimile, or image) both within a country and between that country and others.

8 Group of Thirty, 1989.

9 For an illustration of how existing regulations restrict the use of cost-reducing satellite technologies, see Dixon (1990).

10 e.g. Hoekman and Leidy, 1991.

On Liberalizing The Capital Account

SPECIAL MERIT AWARD

Summary

It is generally agreed that the full benefits of integration into the world economy accrue only after the capital account has been opened. Nevertheless, many countries remain reluctant to liberalise, and the literature on the sequencing of economic reform—which recommends that the capital account should be the last thing to be liberalized in a reform program—may provide a rationalization for this reluctance.

It happens that all preconditions for liberalization developed in the sequencing literature provide reasons for delaying liberalization of capital *inflows* rather than of all capital movements. This essay addresses the complementary issue of the preconditions for liberalization of capital *outflows*, a measure that, for reasons explored in the paper, will normally be introduced only after inflows have been liberalized. It is argued that the liberalization program should not be guided by an attempt to fine tune the capital account. Rather, the key issues are identified as (1) a country's acceptance into the community of market-oriented, democratic states, which gives credibility to assurances that the policy regime will not be changed arbitrarily under adverse circumstances, and (2) adequate flexibility of policy instruments to cope with a high degree of capital mobility, meaning either a willingness to accept a flexible exchange rate or a degree of flexibility in fiscal policy.

John Williamson is a Senior Fellow at the Institute for International Economics, Washington DC. He was formerly professor of economics at Pontificia Universidade Catolica do Rio de Janeiro, University of Warwick, Massachusetts Institute of Technology, University of York, and Princeton University; Advisor to the International Monetary Fund; and Economic Consultant to Her Majesty's Treasury. He has published a number of works on a wide range of international economic issues, including most recently *The Economic Opening of Eastern Europe*, and (with Chris Milner) *The World Economy: A Textbook in International Economics.*

10

On Liberalizing The Capital Account

JOHN WILLIAMSON

Standard economic theory explains that the full benefits of integration into the world economy accrue only after a country has liberalized the capital account of its balance of payments as well as the current account. Only then can investment be pushed to the optimal level independently of any constraint posed by domestic savings, and only then can savings be deployed to best advantage so as to achieve full risk diversification.

While the benefits of such integration are rarely challenged today there remains concern about the dangers of premature liberalization. This is best exemplified by the literature about 'sequencing', which argues that the capital account should be the last thing to be free in a program of economic liberalization.

This conclusion is reinforced rather than contested in the present paper. It is argued that the preconditions identified in the sequencing literature apply only to the freeing of capital inflows, and that a separate set of preconditions should be required prior to the liberalization of outflows. The paper starts with a brief review of the sequencing literature, and then proceeds to elaborate the set of preconditions that seem called for prior to abolishing controls on outflows. It concludes by summarizing the strategy recommended for overall liberalization of the capital account.

The Sequencing Literature

Following the failure of the Southern Cone liberalization programs of the late 1970s, a number of economists asked whether the failure might be explicable by inappropriate ordering of the sequence in which different markets were liberalized,[1] rather than by the objective of liberalization itself being misplaced. The literature on sequencing is in some respects still inconclusive, but it does seem to have been widely agreed that the capital account should be liberalized last.

Four reasons have been given for this recommendation. The first assumes that liberalization of the capital account induces a capital inflow, which causes an appreciation of the currency, which undermines the competitiveness of the tradable goods industries, and thus brings export-led growth to a standstill and in due course threatens the country with renewed financial crisis. Second, importing capital before fiscal discipline has been established may simply permit the maintenance of unsustainable budget deficits for a time, again sowing the seeds of a future crisis. The third reason argues that capital which flows in before trade has been liberalized may go into the wrong industries, causing immiserizing growth. Similarly, capital that flows in before the financial system has been liberalized may be inefficiently allocated. (It is of course widely recognized today that financial liberalization has its own precondition, namely strong prudential supervision.) Hence the conclusion is that liberalization of the capital account should be delayed until nontraditional export industries are well-established and fiscal discipline is secure, and until both trade and the financial system have been liberalized.

Although the literature speaks of 'liberalizing the capital account', all four of the above conditions are designed to avoid problems from an excessive *inflow* of capital. They are indeed very sensible conditions to require before liberalizing capital inflows. But their presence does not necessarily imply that it is a good idea to liberalize the *outflow* of capital. Whether that is advisable demands a separate analysis.

Costs and Benefits of Liberalizing Outflows

The first thing that policy-makers usually worry about when it is suggested that capital outflows should be liberalized is that this will reduce the volume of domestic investment. Domestic savings will be placed abroad instead of invested at home, and in consequence growth will decline. In particular, there is reluctance to risk losing the limited stock of funds available for long-term investment, such as those controlled by pension funds.

Experience with capital flight would suggest that this effect has to be taken seriously. True, it is sometimes argued or implied that capital controls are so porous that their removal would do little to increase the export of capital. However, the mere fact that it is always possible for wealth-owners to place their funds abroad retail, at a premium through a parallel market, does not imply that controls that prevent institutions exporting capital wholesale, at the official rate, are ineffective in limiting the export of capital. It is certainly true that capital controls can prevent the placement abroad of long-term institutional savings. It is also true that capital controls can slow the process of capital export, thus giving the authorities time to react to incipient capital flight before it is too late. Assertions about the ineffectiveness of capital controls are vastly exaggerated.

What is certainly true is that in some instances (Britain in 1979, or Yugoslavia in 1990) the removal of capital outflow controls had the paradoxical effect of stimulating a net *inflow* of capital, presumably by bolstering confidence and assuring investors that it would be easy to get their money out again should they so wish. This is, however, a result on which it would surely be unwise to rely: it is the sort of effect that seems likely to be present just as long as it is not needed to achieve the objectives of policy. (Yugoslavia saw its capital inflow reverse strongly only nine months after liberalizing outflows, and reimposed controls after a further two months.) Moreover, there is no evidence that removing outflow controls prompts an inflow of the sort of stable, long-term investment funds that are a particular source of concern.

On the other hand, policy-makers sometimes look to capital outflows to resolve a problem of excessive reserve accumulation that they fear will subvert their efforts to maintain an exchange rate sufficiently competitive to promote continued investment in the tradable goods industries, and thus perpetuate export-led growth. Note that a gain from this source can arise only if several conditions are satisfied: the level of investment must be constrained by the propensity to invest rather than by the level of savings (contrary to the presumption implicit in the discussion preceding this paragraph); the liberalization of capital outflows must actually cause a net incipient capital outflow, rather than a net inflow due to the boost to confidence as discussed above; and the authorities must permit a change in incipient capital flows to cause a change in the exchange rate.

So what do these considerations suggest about the desirability of abolishing controls on capital outflows? Countries with a chronic savings shortage and great uncertainty, like those in Eastern Europe today, would run a risk of capital flight if they were to liberalize now.

They need to keep their savings at home during the period of reconstruction that lies ahead—like the countries of Western Europe and East Asia did in similar circumstances (and in contrast to the countries of Latin America over the past decade). But once countries get beyond that point (as today in much of East Asia and in a few of the more successful Latin American countries, like Chile, it is impossible to know whether a relaxation of capital outflow controls is more likely to cause a net outflow rather than a net inflow, nor be sure whether a net inflow is more likely to raise the level of investment than a net outflow. Under these conditions it would be foolish to determine policy by an attempt to fine tune the flow of capital. Thus a first conclusion is that *removal of capital outflow controls should not be viewed as part of a strategy for trying to fine tune the flow of capital.*

Another cost of abolishing capital controls arises if the flow of capital adjusts perversely to the state of the economy. Specifically, it is often feared, especially in developing countries that are critically dependent on primary product exports, that capital flows may accentuate cyclical instability. A fall in the price of a staple export product might erode confidence and so prompt a capital outflow that would accentuate the recessionary impact of the low export price.

This has certainly been known to happen. On the other hand, it is wrong to think of it as a natural and ineluctable element of the economic order. In developed countries we think of one of the benefits of capital mobility as the ability that it gives us to borrow in difficult times and so to smooth out cyclical shocks. The reason this is possible is that investors have confidence in the permanence of the policy regime.

A well-known benefit of capital mobility is that it permits gains from portfolio diversification. An investor resident in any small economy whose portfolio is confined to domestic assets runs substantially more risk than one who can invest in an international portfolio. This is a source of gain that seems of particular importance to such institutions as pension funds. Foreign investors, in contrast, can be expected to be willing to place a small part of their portfolio in local assets if offered a modest premium on their expected rate of return (a presumption that has received dramatic confirmation from the explosion in equity investment in emerging markets in recent years), provided that the risks they run are only the economic risks inherent in local investments. Hence the potential exists for mutual gain through two-way investment that diversifies the portfolios of both parties, with local investors gaining greater security for a modest cost in lower expected yields, and the foreign investors gaining a greater expected yield for a modest cost in terms of less security.

A problem may arise, however, if the economic risks of investing in the local economy are supplemented by political risks specific to foreign investors. Such risks can easily eliminate the prospect of mutual gain through portfolio diversification. Once again, therefore, the condition for capital mobility to yield a social gain is that investors should have confidence in the permanence of a policy regime that will respect their property rights. This suggests that *the time to dismantle capital controls is when a country has been accepted as a member of the community of market-oriented, democratic states that can be relied on to maintain the policy regime even in the face of difficulties.* Up to now the set of states with such credibility has been practically coterminous with the membership of the OECD.

A further often-cited disadvantage of high capital mobility is that it erodes the effectiveness of monetary policy as an instrument to manage the domestic economy under a regime of fixed (or managed) exchange rates. In the classic case of perfect capital mobility and a fixed exchange rate, it is well known that the central bank loses all power to influence domestic economic conditions (Mundell 1968, ch. 18). In practice capital mobility is never perfect and so the monetary instrument is not totally lost. As long as capital mobility is less than perfect, a restrictive (or expansionary) monetary policy can still be used to restrain (or stimulate) demand, but at a cost that is greater the higher the degree of capital mobility. Chile's experience in restraining demand in 1990 provides a good example: demand was in due course curbed as desired, but this proved extremely expensive to the central bank (which issued a large volume of long-term, high interest bonds in exchange for funds on which it could earn only a much lower interest rate). Chile's ability to restrain demand was doubtless enhanced by the fact that its exchange rate is not completely fixed: Chile currently operates a wide band policy which gives a certain latitude for the exchange rate to vary in response to monetary policy (and, conversely, for monetary policy to vary without violating the announced exchange rate policy). It would nonetheless be unrealistic to imagine that a dismantling of capital controls would not have a price in terms of limiting the effectiveness (or raising the cost) of monetary policy, unless Chile were prepared to abandon its current exchange rate policy in favour of floating.

This cost is important in many countries, because policy instrument, are typically overcommitted. If the authorities wish to maintain a competitive exchange rate so as to support the growth of exports, and also have a rough target for the real interest rate so as to maintain some control over domestic demand, capital controls can help reconcile the two. Hence *the time to dismantle capital controls will be when a new policy instrument becomes available.* That could take the form of a floating exchange rate, although that is a solution that risks jeopardizing the ability to maintain sufficient competitiveness to support the growth of exports. It might also take the form of a more activist fiscal policy, to provide another instrument to manage domestic demand and so release the interest rate for the partial[2] purpose of exchange rate management. Of course, an activist fiscal policy can be relied on to operate in a classic Keynesian stabilizing fashion only when the government is unambiguously solvent, which again limits the countries that are eligible.

Another objection to the liberalization of capital outflows is that the government's captive source of financing for its debt will disappear. This is a weak argument in anything but the very short term. The ability of a government to finance its deficit in competition with other borrowers does not prove that the deficit is not too large, but an inability to finance it without captive sources surely demonstrates that it is excessive.

A more substantive problem with capital outflows is that they may erode the tax base. If a country applies the residence principle of taxation, interest or other income earned from the holding of foreign assets is legally liable to taxation. A problem nonetheless arises from the difficulty of enforcing tax obligations on income earned abroad. In the absence of tax information-sharing agreements with the major industrial countries, a tax on income earned abroad is largely voluntary. Thus in order to limit erosion of the tax base and perhaps also to prevent the pre-tax interest rate abroad becoming the floor for the post-tax interest rate at home, it may be decided to try and prevent domestic capital going abroad at all. Conversely, the abolition of capital outflow controls would open the door to tax evasion and raise domestic interest rates.

It seems to be generally assumed that nothing much can be done to address this problem. This may be too pessimistic. The US Treasury concluded the first tax information-sharing agreement with a Latin American country in late 1989, with Mexico, and let it be known that it would be willing to sign similar agreements with other countries. Admittedly the terms are somewhat limited, since the US authorities provide information only in response to a request as to the earnings of a named individual at a named financial institution. Moreover, it would be easy for an individual to move his account to another country if he felt a strong interest in doing so. Despite these qualifications, the agreement should be regarded as a significant first step (and the significant reflux of flight capital to Mexico since it was signed may have been helped by its existence). Furthermore, the OECD negotiated a multilateral tax information-sharing agreement in 1988–89, which is due to enter into force as soon as one more country ratifies it.[3] Unfortunately participation in this agreement is restricted to members of the OECD and the Council of Europe. There is an obvious need to permit other countries to participate—a move that should also benefit the members of the OECD, since it would further circumscribe the possibilities of their residents evading taxation.

Tax considerations thus suggest that the right time to liberalize capital outflows is *when participation in a multilateral tax information-sharing agreement becomes possible.*

A country with major foreign assets reaps an obvious and surely important benefit from liberalizing the export of capital: liberalization privatizes decisions regarding foreign investment. This factor becomes increasingly important as a country progresses through the debt cycle, which surely helps explain why inflows are typically liberalized before outflows. It suggests that the time to liberalize is *when substantial foreign assets have been accumulated.*

It is also argued that outward investment should be liberalized because some foreign investments, notably direct investments, are likely to have particularly high yields. This suggests that outward flows of direct investment should be liberalized early, but it does not need the abolition of all controls on outward investment to accomplish this.

Another source of gain from the abolition of controls on capital outflows is a saving in public expenditure. (Britain's abolition of capital controls released about one quarter of the staff of the Bank of England, plus those who formerly had to negotiate with them in the private sector.) It is increasingly difficult to keep an economy's capital markets insulated as its goods markets become ever more closely integrated into the world economy in order to achieve the full benefits offered by trade. The more extensive are trade links, the greater is the need to provide trade credit and to create foreign subsidiaries to support export sales, while the more difficult and therefore costly it becomes to control the capital account because of the multiplication in the number of arbitrage possibilities created in the course of normal business. Hence it is only realistic to recognize that in a growing economy the ability to impose effective capital outflow controls will erode progressively. Thus the question is not whether to liberalize outflows, but when.

A Strategy for Liberalization

The 'globalization of financial markets', a somewhat hyperbolic phrase for the integration of the financial markets of the developed countries, is surely here for good, in two senses: it would be impractical to reverse it, and it would be foolish to try even if it were feasible. Other countries can be expected to liberalize their capital controls and join the 'global financial market' in due course. But that does not imply that every country should be urged to liberalize its capital account without more ado. As already recognized in the sequencing literature, capital controls should be abolished only after a number of preconditions have been established.

The necessary preconditions are different for the liberalization of capital inflows and outflows. Before liberalizing inflows it is desirable to undertake the sort of reforms that provide the focus of World Bank structural adjustment lending—ensure that non-traditional export industries are firmly established and that fiscal discipline is in place, liberalize the import regime and the financial system (which in turn requires adequate prudential supervision). Once these conditions are satisfied, restrictions on capital inflows can be lifted. This will enable a country to borrow from abroad so as to free the level of domestic investment from the constraint constituted by its own level of domestic savings, which is the important gain offered by capital mobility for a country at an early stage of the debt cycle and in the process of catching up with the industrialized countries.

Some of the benefits of free capital outflows come only at a later stage of the development process as foreign assets accumulate and it is increasingly desirable that these be managed by the private sector, with a view *inter alia* to risk diversification, rather than locked up in low-yielding international reserves. Moreover, the costs of freeing capital outflows are ones that can be finessed when a country can credibly commit itself to maintaining a policy regime unchanged even under adverse circumstances, and when it gains a measure of freedom to use fiscal policy in a stabilizing way. But these are much more demanding conditions than the preconditions for the liberalization of inflows. Hence it is not surprising that most countries have liberalized capital outflows only after inflows were freed.

It was argued that, once the danger of capital flight is past, it would be an error to be guided by ambitions to manipulate the flow of capital in deciding whether and when to liberalize outflows. The right criteria are more fundamental: a policy regime that investors regard as permanent, ability to manage demand by a measure of fiscal flexibility, and arrangements to limit erosion of the tax base.

Perhaps the most critical condition, and surely the most difficult to satisfy, is the establishment of credibility in the permanence of the policy regime. Consider the case of Chile, a country where the possibility of liberalizing outflows of capital is currently a live issue. If Chile were located in Europe, everyone would regard its current policy regime as natural and therefore unlikely to be reversed. But geography is not irrelevant to geoeconomic perceptions, and the combination of Chile's geographical location and the turbulence of its recent political past must create doubts about whether its current policy regime will be maintained in the long run. That could make an immediate dismantling of the remaining capital controls hazardous. If Chile wants to be able to liberalize capital outflows without undue risks, it might start by seeking membership in the OECD, in the hope that this would make credible its intention of perpetuating its present policy regime. This would also have the advantage of securing Chile access to the multilateral OECD tax information-sharing agreement.

A liberalized capital account is a sensible objective that is badly served by demands for the immediate and total abolition of capital controls irrespective of circumstances. Countries have suffered enormously from premature liberalization of both inflows and outflows. This has already been recognised in the sequencing literature, but that deals with only half of the question. It has been argued that the full sequence should be: make the reforms called for by World Bank structural adjustment loans; liberalize capital inflows; make the reforms needed to be a good member of the OECD; join the OECD; liberalize outflows.

References

Edwards, Sebastian (1984), *The Order of Liberalization of the External Sector in Developing Countries,* Princeton Essays in International Finance no.156.
Harberger, Arnold C. (1984), ed., *World Economic Growth* (San Francisco: Institute for Contemporary Studies Press).
McKinnon, Ronald I. (1982), 'The Order of Economic Liberalization: Lessons from Chile', in *Carnegie-Rochester Conference Series on Public Policy.*
Mundell, Robert A. (1968), *International Economics* (London: Macmillan).

Notes

1 The major contributors to this literature were Edwards (1984), Krueger in Harberger (1984), and McKinnon (1982).
2 A wide band can still give some scope to allow the interest rate a role in managing domestic demand.
3 Finland, Norway, Sweden and most recently the United States have already ratified, and the agreement enters into force as soon as it has been ratified by five countries.

Money is Funny, or Why Finance is Too Complex for Physics

SPECIAL MERIT AWARD

Summary

Virtually all conventional theoretical models of economic phenomena and, perforce, all mainline academic models of finance, rest upon a metaphor drawn from classical physics. The dialogue presented here shows why such mathematical and computational pictures of the world of finance—including even the newest metaphors from modern physics involving such things as chaotic processes—are forever doomed to fail as valid portrayals of the way *real* investors behave and the way *real* financial markets operate. The conclusion emerging from these deliberations is that financial modellers would be far better off consulting a biology book than a physics text for their metaphorical inspirations—finance is just too complex for physics.

John L. Casti is a Professor of Econometrics, Operations Research and System Theory at the Technical University of Vienna, Austria. Following completion of a doctorate in Mathematics from the University of Southern California in 1970, he served on the faculties of New York University and Princeton before joining the research staff of the International Institute for Applied Systems Analysis (IIASA) in Vienna in early 1974. He served at IIASA until October 1986, at which time he joined the faculty of the Technical University. His current research interests centre on the development of biologically-based mathematical representations of economic and other social phenomena. He is the author of over 100 research articles and eight technical monographs. In addition, he has recently written *Paradigms Lost* and *Searching for Certainty* (Morrow, New York, 1989, 1991 and Scribners, London, 1990, 1992), general-readership volumes addressing major unsolved problems in science and the limitations of science as a mechanism for the prediction and explanation of everyday events.

11

Money is Funny, or Why Finance is Too Complex for Physics*

JOHN L. CASTI

The Scene

EVENT: The annual meeting of the Transworld Society for Science, Truth and Beauty in Modelling

DATE: Sometime in the very near future

SETTING: A panel discussion on 'Mathematical and Computer Modelling of Economic and Financial Processes—Science or Alchemy'?

THEME: Is physics a suitable metaphor upon which to base models aimed at explaining and/or predicting the behaviour of price movements on speculative markets?

Dramatis Personae

Professor Ransom ('Randy') Walker: guru of mainline academic finance and devotee of efficient markets and rational expectations; renegade theoretical physicist turned financial analyst.

Mr D. O. W. Jones: representative from the Association of International Investment Fund Managers; training in philosophy, with an MBA in finance.

Professor Max U. Till: Viennese-born and educated behavioural psychologist; well known for his experimental work on the identification of how real people make real financial decisions in real market environments.

Col. Hy R. Fees: big-time stocks-and-commodities broker, a man with no formal academic training whatsoever, but an expert in making 'the right connections' (and lots of money).

* The author wishes to thank William Brock, Willi Okresek and Maya Weil for helpful discussions of an earlier draft of this essay.

150   John L. Casti

Dame Bea Wright: avant-garde systems thinker, modeller, intellectual
gadfly and general iconoclast; originally trained as a mathematician
and computer scientist, but now working as a theoretical biologist and
philosopher of science.

Panel Moderator.

The Panel Discussion

Moderator: Near the end of the Second Epilogue of War and
               Peace, Tolstoy remarks that 'Only by taking an
               infinitesimally small unit for observation (the differen-
               tial of history, that is, the individual tendencies of
               men) and attaining to the art of integrating them (that
               is, finding the sum of these infinitesimals) can we hope
               to arrive at the laws of history.' Of course, in writing
               this passage Tolstoy was merely echoing the scientific
               attitude of his day, one anchored firmly in the clock-
               work picture of the progression of worldly affairs
               bequeathed to us by Newton, and enshrined in
               Newton's famous laws of motion governing the
               behaviour of material bodies. But to my eye it looks as
               if by substituting the word 'finance' for 'history',
               Tolstoy's statement would serve equally well as a
               research manifesto for the mathematical and computer
               modelling branch of the academic finance community.
               Perhaps Professor Walker would care to open our dis-
               cussion by commenting on this?
Prof. Walker: I don't think any of us here would deny that all eco-
               nomic activity ultimately rests on the 'individual ten-
               dencies of men', to use the phrase from Tolstoy's
               elegant formulation. And it is certainly a truism that
               the sum total of all these individual decisions and
               actions is exactly what ends up determining the price
               of a share of stock or a barrel of oil. But financial mod-
               ellers have come a long way since the time of
               Newton—and since the time of Tolstoy, too, for that
               matter.
                  In the 1960s financial theorists discovered earlier
               work by the Frenchman Louis Bachelier, who around

the turn of the century was the first to study mathematically the properties of price changes of a speculative commodity. Bachelier's ideas led to what we now call the 'random walk hypothesis'. This is the claim that price changes for any commodity fluctuate randomly. As a result, theorists claim that a history of such price information cannot serve as the basis for any kind of trading scheme, or rule, that can consistently outperform the market as a whole, measured by, say, something like the S&P 500 index of stock prices on the New York exchanges. 'Souping up' the random-walk theory by adding the notion of an 'efficient market', which rests upon a behavioural assumption about the way investors make decisions, modern financial theorists have strengthened Bachelier's ideas into the so-called *efficient market hypothesis (EMH)*. Put simply, the EMH states that no publicly available information of any kind can form the basis for a trading rule that will regularly beat the market over a long period of time.

Moderator: But doesn't the EMH rest on assumptions that are just translations into financial terms of many of the very same assumptions underlying the Newtonian models of how material objects like planets and billiard balls behave?

Prof. Walker: Speaking as a former physicist, I can hardly deny that. The hypothesis of market efficiency is basically an equilibrium assumption, saying that investors behave so that any imbalance in supply and demand generated by new information coming into the market is immediately counteracted. This kind of negative feedback effect then acts to generate price movements that tend to push prices toward a single, global, stable equilibrium level at which both buyers and sellers are satisfied. And such a single, stable equilibrium is definitely a central aspect of the Newtonian picture of the movement of material bodies.

Furthermore, the EMH assumes that all investors act in a purely rational manner on the basis of their expectations of future prices. More specifically, the assumption is that each investor forms an estimate of tomorrow's price, and then acts today so as to maximize his or her expected marginal return. So, speaking loosely, you might say that the rational expectations assumption is a finance-world version of the principle of minimal energy governing the behaviour of a system of Newtonian particles.

And, of course, the essence of the whole EMH idea is that finance is not a historical process, in the sense that the particular path taken in arriving at today's price has no influence whatsoever on what will happen tomorrow—just like tomorrow's position of the moon is determined only by where it is today and not how it came to be in this location. So if you want to think that these features of the EMH suggest a kind of physics-envy on the part of academic finance theorists, you have my blessing. After all, why shouldn't we base our models on those of physics? They are by far the most well-developed, coherent and successful set of theories we humans have ever created for describing in scientific terms the way the world seems to work.

Mr Jones: Maybe these theories do a good job of describing the worlds of black holes, planets, quarks and billiard balls. But if you'll pardon the neologism, those Newtonian notions don't seem to fit my world of *Realfinanz*, at all. In this world I see as much irrationality and 'groupthink' as I do cool, calculated, rational behaviour. Personally, I think this rational expectations business is a lot of abstract 'π in the sky' invented by you professors of finance to debate at academic conventions and write scholarly articles about. I don't think it makes one bit of contact with the way things actually work on the floor of the exchange.

Col. Fees: Hrumph! Hrumph! I dare say old boy I'm forced to agree with you. A number of my clients are real boffins, frightfully good chaps with numbers, formulas and that sort of thing. And some of them have told me about various stock market anomalies, things like the Value Line enigma, the low price/earnings effect and the small-firms phenomenon, each of which certainly

seems to put the lie to the EMH. Why, one of my
American clients even says he can forecast the long-
term movement of the market using the outcome of
their Super Bowl football game, whatever that is.
Some sort of American rugby, I gather, not real football at all. The fellow's slightly barmy, if you ask me.
Nevertheless, he swears that this Super Bowl indicator
works over 90 per cent of the time. But even if it
doesn't, I can hardly think of a more irrational scheme
for betting, err . . . I mean investing, on the market.
How can football scores have anything to do with
stock prices? Sounds like a lot of claptrap to me.
Complete rubbish!

Moderator: Hmm, yes. Ah . . . thank you very much, Colonel Fees.
Let me shift the discussion for a moment to one of the
most exciting new scientific ideas to hit the world of
theoretical finance since the random-walk theory. Of
course, I'm referring to the claim that price changes
follow what the mathematicians call a 'chaotic' rule. A
lot of edge-of-the-frontier financial thinkers currently
seem to believe that there really do exist definite rules,
or recipes, according to which price histories are generated in a fixed, even deterministic way. But the problem is that whatever the precise form of these rules
may be, the result of applying such a rule to past prices
leads to a chaotic, 'incompressible' sequence of numbers. So, although a definite rule for price changes may
indeed exist, we could never hope to make use of it in
any practical way to predict the future course of price
movements.

Mr Jones: Why not? If we know the rule, then it should be
straightforward to employ it to calculate what the markets will be doing next.

Moderator: The reason why such a chaotic rule cannot be applied
to past price changes in order to predict future ones is
that the outcome of following such a rule is pathologi-
cally sensitive to any errors we make in measuring the
past price information or in carrying out the computations called for by the rule. In the language of physics,
this kind of prescription for price changes is unstable

in the worst possible way. So even if we knew the exact form of the rule (which we most assuredly do not), since data is almost always known imprecisely and computations are carried out only to a fixed degree of precision, the predictions obtained from following this kind of chaotic rule rapidly degenerate to meaningless nonsense. Ironically, this unpredictability of price changes is just what the random-walk theory claims, too—but for very different reasons. However, even if there is some magical chaotic rule that really is the one true mechanism by which market prices fluctuate, I still wonder how it fits in with the deeper issue of whether physics—classical or chaotic—is a suitable metaphor upon which to build valid models of the behaviour of financial markets. I know that Dame Wright holds some rather definite views on this matter.

Dame Wright: Indeed. To mathematically represent price changes with a model displaying chaotic behaviour, thereby thinking you're making progress in financial modelling, is like thinking you're making progress in getting to the moon by going out into your garden and climbing a tree. Both show the same singular lack of understanding of the basic nature of the problem.

Chaotic dynamical processes depart in no essential way from the Newtonian paradigm of a clockwork universe. Their only novel feature, and the source of all the recent brouhaha about 'chaos' in the popular and scientific press, is that they display a new type of long-run behaviour quite unlike that shown by more traditional dynamical processes. Classical Newtonian systems have two types of long-run behaviour: (1) an equilibrium point of the type a marble rolling around inside a soup bowl ends up at, or (2) a periodic orbit like the path the Earth takes in its annual tour around the Sun.

In addition to these classical types of 'attractors', which were known even in Newton's time, chaotic processes can show a third type of long-run behaviour called a 'strange attractor'. Instead of being points or closed orbits, strange attractors look a lot like a bowl-

ful of spaghetti. This means that small, perhaps un-
measurable—or even unknowable—disturbances to
the system can push the system trajectory from moving along one strand of spaghetti to motion along
another. And in this way the process goes off onto an
entirely different course of behaviour. As our moderator already mentioned, it's this almost pathological
type of sensitivity to disturbances that gives rise to the
great difficulties we have in predicting what a chaotic
system will do next. But the underlying framework is
still resolutely Newtonian—and in exactly the sense
we spoke of earlier. All that's been added to Newton's
picture is this third type of attractor.

Prof. Walker: Perhaps Dame Wright would care to enlighten us by
spelling out just what she thinks a proper, 21st-century
non-Newtonian framework for modelling financial
processes should look like?

Dame Wright: I'm glad you asked that question, Professor Walker.
Earlier you told us that EMH-oriented financial theorists regard finance as a non-historical science. I often
wonder how professors of finance can make such
statements with a straight face. It doesn't take much by
way of deep analysis of the literature or detailed study
of the behaviour of actual markets to see that this can't
possibly be the case. Future price changes are dramatically affected by the particular path a market has taken
in getting to its present level. For example, if the SP
500 index stands at 370 today, it's ludicrous to think
that tomorrow's level doesn't depend in crucially
important ways on exactly what path events took leading up to the index being at this level. I think anyone
with even a modicum of street smarts will tell you that
if the 370 level is reached in a climate of steadily rising interest rates and unemployment, that's a totally
different story than seeing the index at 370 against a
background of declining interest rates and increasing
consumer confidence. The big run-up in stock prices in
early 1991 following the Gulf War is a perfect example illustrating the point. Of course, EMH advocates have
constructed many devious schemes to try to circumvent

this glaring deficiency in their financial *Weltanschau-ung*. But you can't sweep the dirt under the rug for ever. Eventually you've got to toss it into the trash barrel. And that means creating a modelling paradigm that's specifically designed for the peculiarities of financial markets and human beings, not billiard balls and planets. So the first feature a non-Newtonian modelling paradigm for finance should display is some kind of provision for path-dependence in its descriptive framework.

Mr Jones: But what about things like market crashes, tulip manias and all the other situations in which rapid, discontinuous shifts in prices occur? Don't you think something like the chaos-type models might be the best way to account scientifically for these kinds of booms and busts?

Dame Wright: Not necessarily. Any dynamical process, chaotic or otherwise, that admits both stable and unstable long-run behaviours can give rise to such rapid, jerky kinds of shifts under appropriate circumstances. And, in fact, if you give me a set of price changes, I'll give you back an infinite set of rules (i.e., models), *all* of which will reproduce your price history exactly. Good models of reality give us genuine *insight* into that reality, not just good agreement with what's been observed. And the business of science is knowing the why of things, not just the what or even the when. So any type of recipe for price movements that merely agrees with observed past price histories is very far from being a 'good' model, at least in a scientific sense.

Prof. Walker: But, but . . .

Dame Wright: Please allow me to finish. I'm not saying that these chaos-based models are necessarily on the wrong track; I'm saying simply that they don't as yet make explicit provision for the sort of *explanatory* features that a good mathematical reflection of market reality should display. Or, at least, what a model should contain if it's to give us any genuine insight into what's happening in these markets and why. For example, not only are the current models inherently non-historical, they are also pitifully inadequate when it comes to their built-in assumptions about the psychology of market participants, as both Mr Jones and Col. Fees have already mentioned in connection with the rational expectations fairy tale.

Moderator: You've raised a vitally important point regarding the way real-life investors behave when faced with real financial decisions. Professor Till is well known for his ingenious experiments aimed at determining just exactly how these real investors do in fact behave when hard cash is on the line. Could you please tell us about some of your findings, Professor?

Prof. Till: Ja. It is my pleasure. We have built a mini-exchange in our laboratory with students playing on this market with real money. What we have discovered is that speculative 'bubbles' frequently occur, even when traders know that the market price is far above the fundamental stock value. These bubbles are caused by inexperienced and over-eager traders. When we try to remove the bubbles by adding futures trading, margin buying, short selling and rules to stop trading when the market falls by a certain amount—what the press calls 'circuit breakers'—we find that only futures trading reduces the size and duration of the bubbles. It's funny that circuit-breaker rules actually make these bubbles bigger and last longer—before the crash.

Col. Fees: Jolly good, Professor. Maybe your results will convince the SEC and other market meddlers that the brokers were right after all, and that these circuit-breaker rules only make markets more volatile, not less.

Mr Jones: Tell us, Professor, what have you discovered about the behaviour patterns of individual traders?

Prof. Till: We have discovered that traders get carried away in rising markets, bidding prices up instead of buying on fundamentals like price/earnings ratios or expected dividends.

We have also made a very important empirical discovery. We found that individuals do *not* maximize utility in the way economists think. Standard theory tells us that an individual makes choices to maximize marginal utility. This means that choices are made so that we tend toward an equilibrium state in which equal increments of satisfaction come from each possible activity. This is the principle of maximising marginal utility. We find that this assumption is completely wrong.

Our experiments show that traders tend to maximise *average* utility, not marginal. What this means is that they use a nonstandard formula to discount time. Standard theory say time is discounted at a constant rate; we find that time is discounted at a *hyperbolic* rate. So rewards not only take on different values at different times in the future, they lose value at different rates too. This kind of discounting predicts that traders will initially act rationally; but eventually they will fail to do so.

Mr Jones: But why would traders follow such a discounting rule? It seems that by doing this they are acting against their own selfish interests, giving up gains that they could have received through maximizing marginal returns in favour of the lower returns they get from this hyperbolic discounting scheme, which maximizes only their average utility.

Prof. Till: Ja. This is the key question. Hyperbolic discounting is nonoptimal—maybe! The problem is with how you measure what is optimal. We think that the solution is that it is much easier to calculate average utility than marginal, just as it's easier to add two numbers than it is to form their difference. So we believe that while marginals are needed for truly rational behaviour, they are hard to compute. Most people lack the information and analytical power to compute them reliably. Also, these marginals are very unstable; a small mistake in the data or in the computation leads to a big error in the end. So we think that over the millenia evolution has favoured the computation of average utility, not marginal. This means that investors, they do not act the way rational expectations theory says.

Moderator: So would you conclude, Professor, that another crucially important feature that a new framework for

	financial modelling should incorporate is some replacement for the rational expectations hypothesis?
Prof. Till:	Jawohl! What we need is some new way to represent how traders really form expectations of the future.
Dame Wright:	Perhaps a helpful way to think about this matter is to say we need to inject a form of self-reference into the paradigm for finance. I think even Professor Walker would agree that every trader has some kind of internal mental model of both the market and himself, which he runs on a time scale faster than real time in order to generate his individual expectation for the future. Our non-Newtonian view of financial markets should explicitly incorporate these self-referential models somehow, as well as include learning procedures by which these models get updated. The rational expectations hypothesis neatly does away with this problem by the crude expedient of just assuming that all traders use the same maximal-marginal-return model for the future and, moreover, that the model is never updated. But we know that not everyone has the same attitudes toward risk, nor do people fail to learn from past experience. So again we find the conventional wisdom of the EMH being more of an academic fantasy than an account of how the players act in any real financial market.
Prof. Walker:	Naturally, we always simplify real-life situations for the sake of arriving at a formulation of the problem that we can work with. It would be totally impractical, if not impossible, for our models to account explicitly for every trader's personal picture of the market and himself. Scientific theories and models are always simplifications of the real thing. And the rational expectations hypothesis is just such a simplification.
Dame Wright:	I think it was Einstein who once remarked, 'A theory should be as simple as possible—but no simpler'. By this, I think what he meant was that what separates a good theory from a bad one lies in the choice of the features of the real situation to include in the theory and what aspects to leave out. In my opinion, the traditional EMH-based models of financial markets, including the

ones based on chaotic dynamics, end up throwing out the baby with the bathwater.

Moderator: Well, I see our time is running short. So I'm afraid I'll have to bring this very thought-provoking discussion to a close. But before doing so, let me try to summarize what's been said here today.

My sense of the discussion is that the conventional physics-based paradigm for modelling the price changes on speculative markets is in deep trouble, epistemologically speaking at least. Some radically new framework, or paradigm, seems to be called for that would, at the bare minimum, incorporate the following features: (1) positive (i.e. deviation-amplifying) feedbacks, thereby admitting the possibility of processes having both stable and unstable modes of long-run behaviours, (2) path-dependence of price changes, (3) new behavioural assumptions replacing the notion of strict rationality, and (4) the self-referential, anticipatory models of individual traders.

When I look at this list of desiderata, I can't help thinking that what we're talking about here is a modelling metaphor that's a lot closer to something we might see in a biology book than what's on offer between the covers of a physics text—classical or modern. Somehow it seems as if the physics-based frameworks are just too simple, in Einstein's sense, for the real world of finance. If we're ever going to get a scientific handle on the ways of financial markets, let alone on the larger universe of social and behavioural phenomena, it looks as if we'll be forced to move away from the realm of the simple systems of physics, and confront complex systems head-on. From what we've heard from the panel today, finance is just too complex for physics.

Now let me thank the participants for taking time today to give us their views on this fascinating topic. Perhaps we can continue this discussion at next year's TSSTBM meeting. Hopefully, by then some of today's discussants, or even some of you in the audience, may have new ideas and research results to share with us about how to deal with the complexities of finance. So until then, I wish you all the best of luck in your individual gropings and copings with complexity—wherever and whenever you stumble over it!